Outlook™ 98

fast & easy

Visit us online at www.primalifestyles.com

Outlook™ 98

fast & easy

Payne Consulting Group, Inc.

PRIMA PUBLISHING

Prima Publishing and colophon are registered trademarks of Prima Communications, Inc. Fast & Easy is a trademark of Prima Communications, Inc. Prima Publishing, Rocklin, California 95677.

Publisher: Matthew H. Carleson
Managing Editor: Dan J. Foster
Acquisitions Editor: Deborah F. Abshier
Senior Editor: Kelli R. Crump
Assistant Project Editor: Kevin W. Ferns
Editorial Assistant: Kim V. Benbow
Copy Editor: Theresa Mathias
Technical Reviewer: Ray Link
Interior Layout: Marian Hartsough
Cover Design: Prima Design Team
Indexer: Katherine Stimson

Microsoft, Windows, and Outlook are either registered trademarks or trademarks of Microsoft Corporation.

Important: If you have problems installing or running Microsoft Outlook 98, notify Microsoft at (425) 635-7056 or on the Web at www.microsoft.com. Prima Publishing cannot provide software support.

Prima Publishing and the authors have attempted throughout this book to distinguish proprietary trademarks from descriptive terms by following the capitalization style used by the manufacturer.

Information contained in this book has been obtained by Prima Publishing from sources believed to be reliable. However, because of the possibility of human or mechanical error by our sources, Prima Publishing, or others, the Publisher does not guarantee the accuracy, adequacy, or completeness of any information and is not responsible for any errors or omissions or the results obtained from the use of such information. Readers should be particularly aware of the fact that the Internet is an ever-changing entity. Some facts may have changed since this book went to press.

ISBN: 0-7615-1405-8
Library of Congress Catalog Card Number: 97-76319
Printed in the United States of America

00 01 HH 10 9 8 7 6 5 4 3

Acknowledgments

We want to thank everyone who worked on this book at Prima Publishing. Acquisitions Editor Debbie Abshier has always been a supporter and friend. Senior Editor Kelli Crump was a pleasure to work with and made the process of writing the book easier and smoother than we could have hoped for. More thanks to Dan Foster, Matt Carlson, Ben Dominitz, Stacey Roberts, and to everyone at Prima who work on each book but don't always receive the credit they deserve—thank you!

Special thanks to the staff at Payne Consulting Group who were not actively involved in writing this book but who offered their assistance when necessary: Robert Affleck, Jill Looper, Kevin Steger, and Chris Thomas. Special thanks to Tara Byers of Payne Consulting Group for reshooting many of the screen shots when a new version of the beta was released!

Very special thanks to our family and friends: Rob, David, and Charis Terray; Robert, Alexis, Janice, and David Affleck; Pam Perrault; Rose and Gary Perkins; Jolynn Webb; Daniel and Thomas Campos; Joy, Matt, and Scott Suttles; Sue Mosher; Allison and Aaron Kelly; Frank Provenzano; Pearl Payne; and Ethel Harding.

About the Authors

Payne Consulting Group, Inc., provides expert training and development services and specializes in Microsoft Office applications. PCG's team of training and development experts are world renowned and Microsoft Certified. They are recognized as leaders in their field, have won multiple awards, and are published authors. Payne Consulting Group is a Microsoft Certified Solution Provider and has four Microsoft Most Valuable Professionals (MVPs) on staff. They have been technical beta testers for Outlook 98 and many Microsoft applications and operating systems. PCG's Web page is at www.payneconsulting.com.

Andrea Terray is Microsoft Certified and a recipient of the Microsoft Most Valuable Professional (MVP) award. She is a training manager for Payne Consulting Group and has taught hundreds of users how to get the most out of Microsoft Office applications. She is co-author of *Word 97 for Law Firms* and has authored magazine articles for computer and home business magazines. She can be reached at andreaterray@dpayne.com.

Donna Payne is President of Payne Consulting Group, Inc. She is a Microsoft Certified Trainer and four-time award recipient of the Microsoft Most Valuable Professional (MVP) award. Donna has developed custom applications and provided training for many internationally based firms. She has authored many books on Microsoft Office, most recently *Word 97 for Law Firms* and *The Essential Excel 97 Book*. Donna has written and been the subject of numerous articles for computer, business, and industry magazines. She can be reached at donnapayne@dpayne.com.

David Webb is Microsoft Certified and a trainer and developer for Payne Consulting Group. David has taught hundreds of end-user classes and is especially experienced in teaching people who are new to computers. In addition to training, David is a developer for Microsoft Office applications and Visual Basic. He can be reached at davidwebb@dpayne.com.

Contents at a Glance

Contents

PART III
SCHEDULING WITH THE CALENDAR 97

PART IX
APPENDIX **277**

Introduction

This new *Fast & Easy* guide from Prima Publishing will help you unleash the power of Microsoft Outlook 98. Outlook is a messaging and contact management program that will allow you to do all of the things other Personal Information Management (PIM) programs do, but it will also make it easier than ever to make your information work together. For example, you can make your contact information work seamlessly with your e-mail messages in Outlook.

Outlook 98 Fast & Easy provides you with all the information you need to begin using the powerful features of Outlook 98 today. As you read this book, you'll tackle many of the features Outlook has to offer. You'll learn at a record pace with the step-by-step approach, clear language, and color illustrations of exactly what you will see on your screen.

WHO SHOULD READ THIS BOOK?

Outlook 98 Fast & Easy is ideal as a learning tool or as a step-by-step task reference. The easy-to-follow, highly visual nature of this book makes it the perfect learning tool for a beginning computer user. Also, veteran computer users who are new to this version of Outlook will find this book helpful.

Current users of Outlook 98 can utilize this book as well when they need occasional reminders about the steps required to perform a particular task. It is designed to cut straight to the chase to provide the information you need without having to sort through pages of dense text.

TIPS FOR GETTING THE MOST FROM THIS BOOK

As you use *Outlook 98 Fast & Easy*, you'll notice it focuses on the steps necessary for a task and keeps explanations to a minimum. Included in the book are some elements that are designed to provide additional information, without encumbering your progress through the steps:

✦ **Tips** provide helpful hints and suggestions for working with features in Outlook 98.

✦ **Notes** give you information about a feature, or comments about how to use a feature effectively in your day-to-day activities.

As an added bonus, the appendix walks you through the Outlook installation process. Refer to it as you install the program for the first time. Finally, the glossary is designed to take the mystery out of Outlook 98 by providing definitions of key terms used throughout the book.

Read and enjoy this book! It is certainly the fastest and easiest way to learn Outlook 98.

PART I
Getting Started with Outlook 98

1 Welcome to Outlook 98

Welcome to Outlook, your electronic tool for managing appointments, addresses, e-mail, and notes. When you first begin using Outlook, you may feel a bit intimidated by all of the buttons, icons, and menus that appear on the screen. Don't worry! After just a few lessons, you will understand and be able to use many of the components of Outlook to organize and simplify your busy life. In this chapter, you'll learn how to:

✦ Start Outlook

✦ Use Outlook for the first time

✦ Exit and log off

STARTING OUTLOOK

1. **Click** on the Windows 95 or Windows NT **Start button** on the Taskbar. The Start menu will appear.

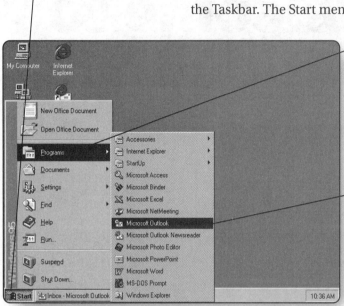

2. **Move** the mouse up to **Programs**. The Programs submenu will appear.

3. **Move** the mouse over to **Microsoft Outlook**. Microsoft Outlook will be highlighted.

4. **Click** on **Microsoft Outlook**. Outlook will open.

TIP

You can also start Outlook by clicking twice (called double-clicking) on the Outlook desktop icon.

NOTE

See the Appendix for more information about creating and selecting a profile.

Working with the Choose Profile Dialog Box

When you install Outlook in a corporate environment, others may use your computer to check their e-mail. Since you don't want their e-mail to be mixed with yours, Outlook provides the ability to create multiple profiles on one machine. It will prompt users to identify themselves by selecting a profile.

If multiple people are using your computer, the Choose Profile dialog box may be enabled and may appear when you start Outlook. If you are the sole user of the computer, Outlook will simply open without presenting the Choose Profile dialog box.

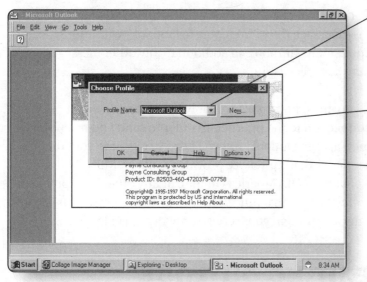

1. **Click** on the **down arrow (▼)** to the right of the Profile Name list box. A drop-down list will appear.

2. **Click** on the **profile** you want. It will be selected.

3. **Click** on **OK**. The Choose Profile dialog box will close and Outlook will open.

USING OUTLOOK FOR THE FIRST TIME

The first time you start Microsoft Outlook, the Office Assistant will appear with helpful messages for new users. You can click on any of the suggested topics to read more about Outlook.

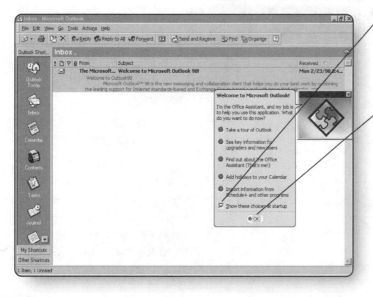

1. **Click** on the **Show these choices at startup check box**. The ✔ will be removed from the check box.

2. **Click** on **OK**. The Office Assistant will close and a dialog box will open, asking if you want to use Word as your e-mail editor.

3. **Click** on the **No button**. Outlook will use its own e-mail editor.

Congratulations! You've just successfully started Outlook. A new message titled "Welcome to Outlook" will automatically appear in your Inbox, in addition to any other messages you may have received.

If you are at home you probably do not have a direct connection to the Internet. In order to send and receive new messages in Outlook, you will need to log on to your dial-up service. A dial-up service provider could be MSN (Microsoft Network), AOL (America Online), or any other local provider. Follow the normal procedure you use for accessing the Internet through your service provider to get logged on.

EXITING OUTLOOK

When you are ready to exit Outlook, you have two choices.

1. **Click** on **File**. The File menu will appear.

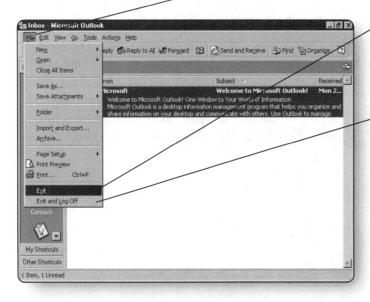

2a. **Click** on **Exit**. You will exit Outlook and remain logged in to your Internet Service Provider.

OR

2b. **Click** on **Exit and Log Off**. You will exit Outlook and log off of your Internet Service Provider.

NOTE

Messages will be delivered to your mailbox when you are logged off. However, you will not see the messages until you log on to your service provider and start Outlook.

2 What's on the Outlook Screen?

Outlook has many features that are used in other Windows-based applications. If you are familiar with these applications, you may already know how to use these features. In this chapter, you'll learn how to:

✦ Use toolbars

✦ Move with scroll bars

✦ Select commands from menus

✦ Explore dialog boxes

UNDERSTANDING THE OUTLOOK ENVIRONMENT

When you first start Outlook, you are presented with the Information viewer. By default, the Information viewer displays the contents of the Inbox. The Inbox stores your incoming e-mail messages.

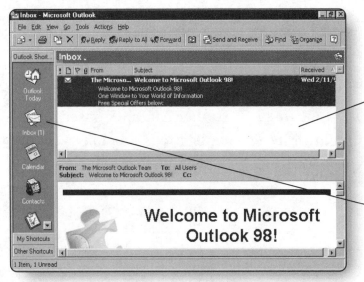

The information displayed in the Information viewer will change depending on which folder is open.

✦ **Information viewer**. The display area for e-mail messages, calendar items, contacts, tasks, journal items, or notes.

✦ **Folders**. Folders are displayed as icons on the Outlook bar. The selected folder's contents will be displayed in the Information viewer.

NOTE

See Chapter 26, "Accessing Frequently Used Commands," for more information.

USING TOOLBARS

Toolbars are located at the top of the Outlook screen. Toolbars contain toolbar buttons; each button represents a commonly used command. Outlook even allows you to customize the toolbars by placing the commands you use most frequently within easy reach.

1. **Move** the **mouse pointer** over any toolbar button. The toolbar button's name will display in a ScreenTip.

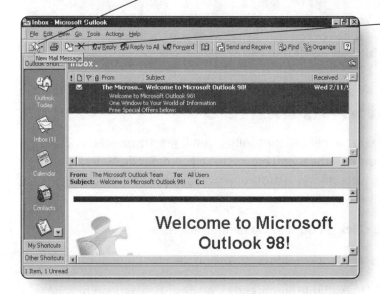

2. **Click** on a **toolbar button**. The command associated with the toolbar button will be executed.

MOVING WITH SCROLL BARS

Scroll bars allow you to change the contents of your screen when there is more information than can fit on one screen. The vertical scroll bar appears on the right edge of the screen, and the horizontal scroll bar appears on the bottom of the screen.

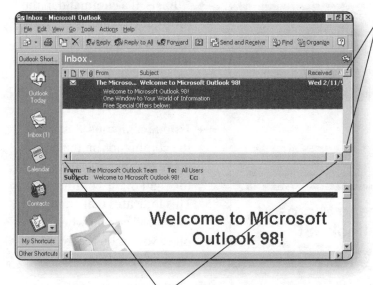

1. **Click** on the **up arrow** (▲) or the **down arrow** (▼) on the vertical scroll bar to move up or down on the screen.

2. **Click** on the **left arrow** (◀) or the **right arrow** (▶) on the horizontal scroll bar to move to the left or right on the screen.

NOTE

If you do not have a horizontal scroll bar, automatic column sizing might be turned on. To turn it off, click on View, Current View, Customize Current View. Click on the Other Settings button, and then click in the check box next to Automatic column sizing to remove the check. Click on OK until all open dialog boxes are closed.

USING MENUS

If you look above the toolbar, you'll see the menu bar. The words on the menu bar are called commands. When you click on a command, a drop-down menu appears containing several other commands.

1. **Click** on **Go**. The Go menu will appear.

There are some things to note on the menu:

✦ **Unavailable commands**. The drop-down menu may have some commands that appear light gray, or dimmed. This means that these commands are not available at this time.

✦ **Ellipsis**. If a command in the drop-down menu is followed by three periods, called an ellipsis, a dialog box will open when you click on the command.

✦ **Extended menus**. Some of the commands on the drop-down menus have an arrow to the right of the command. This indicates that another menu will appear when you place your mouse over or click on the command.

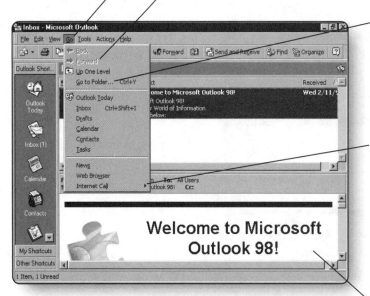

2. **Click anywhere** in the Information viewer. The menu will close.

3. **Click** on another **command** in the menu bar. A drop-down menu will appear.

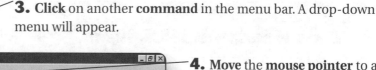

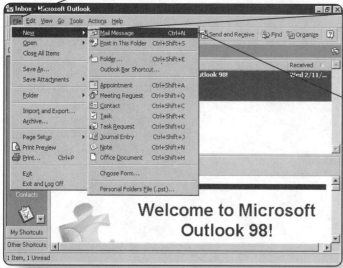

4. **Move** the **mouse pointer** to a command that has a right pointing arrow. The submenu will appear.

5. **Click** on the **command** you want to perform. The associated action will occur.

TIP

You can use the keyboard to select commands rather than the mouse. Simply hold down the Alt key on the keyboard and press the letter corresponding to the underlined character in the command. For example, to open the File menu, press and hold down Alt and F on the keyboard.

EXPLORING DIALOG BOXES

Dialog boxes are windows that appear on the screen asking for more information.

1. **Click** on **File**. The File menu will appear.

2. **Click** on **Print**. The Print dialog box will open.

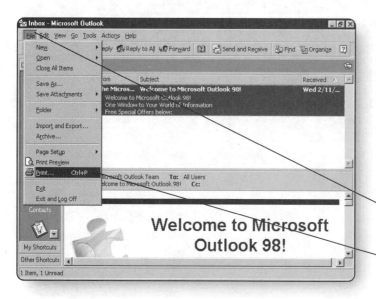

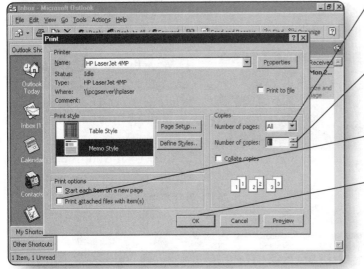

◆ **Click** on a **down arrow (▼)** to make a selection from a drop-down list.

◆ **Click** on the **up** and **down arrows (♦)** to increase or decrease a number.

◆ **Click** in a **check box** to turn on or off a feature.

◆ **Click** on **OK** to close the dialog box and perform the command.

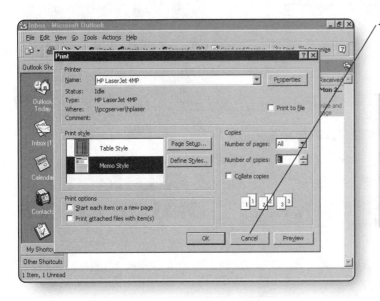

◆ **Click** on **Cancel** to exit the dialog box without performing the command.

TIP

Press the Esc key on the keyboard to cancel a dialog box, or click on the Close button in the upper-right corner of the dialog box.

3 Finding Your Way Around

The way you use Outlook may not be the same way someone else uses the program. Fortunately, Outlook has several options for displaying information. In this chapter, you'll learn how to:

✦ Use the Outlook bar

✦ Display the Folder list

✦ Use Outlook Today

✦ Understand the Outlook icons

USING THE OUTLOOK BAR

The Outlook bar is the gray column located on the left side of the screen. The Outlook bar contains icons that allow you to change what is displayed in the Information viewer. Each icon represents a shortcut to a folder. When you first start Outlook, the Information viewer displays the contents of the Inbox folder.

> **NOTE**
>
> The Outlook bar can be toggled on or off. If you do not see the Outlook bar, click on View, and then click on Outlook bar. A ✔ will appear next to the Outlook bar if it is displayed.

1. **Click** on any **icon**. The items associated with the icon will appear in the Information viewer.

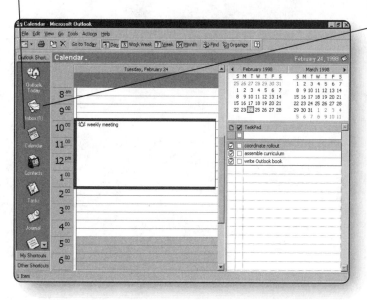

2. **Click** on the **Inbox icon**. E-mail messages will appear again.

There are many icons on the Outlook bar that are not immediately visible. You can click on the scroll bar arrows to see more icons, or switch to a different Outlook group. The default Outlook groups are Outlook Shortcuts, My Shortcuts, and Other Shortcuts.

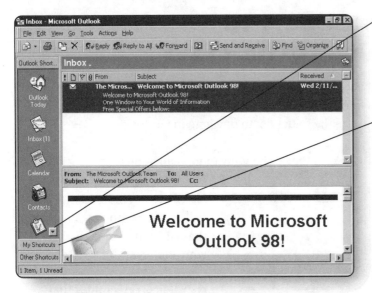

✦ **Outlook scroll bar arrows**. Click on the up or down arrow at the top or bottom of the Outlook bar to scroll up or down.

✦ **Outlook bar group buttons**. Click on an Outlook group button to display different icons.

NOTE

An Outlook group is a way to organize folders on the Outlook bar. You can add, delete, or rename the Outlook groups by clicking the right mouse button on the Outlook bar and clicking on one of the options on the shortcut menu.

You can make the icons on the Outlook bar larger or smaller, depending on your preference.

3. **Click** on the **right mouse button** in a gray area of the Outlook bar. A shortcut menu will appear.

4. **Click** on **Small Icons** with the left mouse button. The size of the icons will be reduced.

DISPLAYING THE FOLDER LIST

The icons that appear on the Outlook bar are also referred to as folders. If you choose not to display the Outlook bar, you can use the folder list to navigate in Outlook.

1. **Click** on **View**. The View menu will appear.

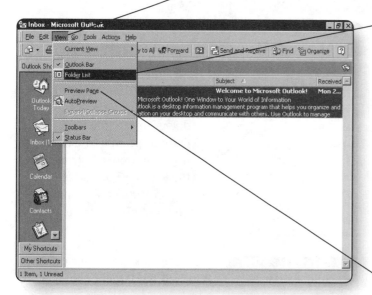

2. **Click** on **Folder List**. A pane will open next to the Outlook bar that will allow you to navigate your folders.

3. **Click** on any **folder** that appears in your folder list. The contents of the selected folder will appear in the Information viewer.

4. **Click** on **Folder List**. The folder list will turn off.

5. **Click** on **Preview Pane**. The preview pane will close.

NOTE

From this point on in the book, you will be working without the preview pane.

USING OUTLOOK TODAY

One of the icons on the Outlook bar is labeled "Outlook Today." Outlook Today displays a snapshot of all of the items you need during the day. Outlook Today also provides quick access to tasks you might frequently perform, such as looking up a particular contact.

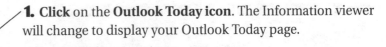

1. Click on the **Outlook Today icon**. The Information viewer will change to display your Outlook Today page.

2. Type a **name** in the Contact text box.

3. Click on **Go** to find a contact. The Find window will open, giving you a list of contacts that match your criteria.

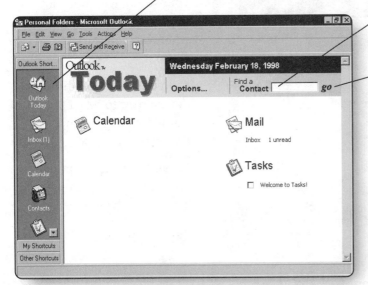

Customizing Outlook Today

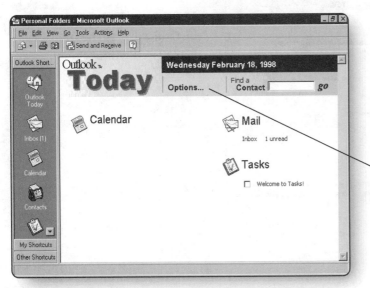

You can customize Outlook Today to display the folders you need, or to adjust the display of the calendar or task list. You can even designate Outlook Today as the default page that appears when Outlook is started.

1. Click on **Options** in the Information viewer. The Outlook Today Options window will appear.

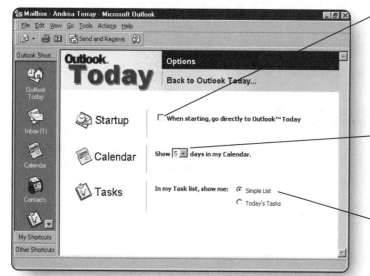

✦ **Startup**. Click on the check box to make Outlook Today your start page. Your start page is what is shown whenever you start up Outlook.

✦ **Calendar**. Click on the drop-down arrow to select the number of days to appear in the calendar.

✦ **Tasks**. Click on an option button to select a simple task list or today's tasks.

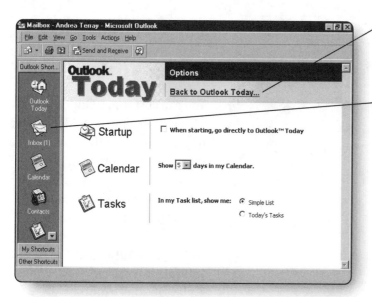

2. **Click** on **Back to Outlook Today**. The Options window will close.

3. **Click** on the **Inbox icon** on the Outlook bar. The Inbox will display in the Information viewer.

UNDERSTANDING OUTLOOK SYMBOLS

Outlook uses numerous symbols to represent different types of items. For example, a red exclamation point is used for high priority items, while a blue down-pointing arrow is used to identify low priority items. Symbols appear next to e-mail messages in the Inbox. You can learn more about the symbols used in Outlook in Outlook Help.

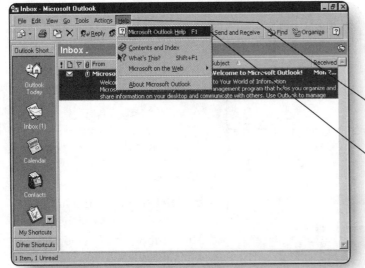

1. **Click** on **Help**. The Help menu will appear.

2. **Click** on **Microsoft Outlook Help**. The Office Assistant will appear.

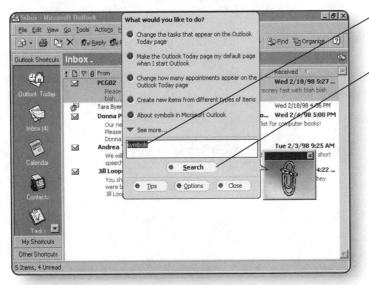

3. **Type** the word **Symbols** in the text box.

4. **Click** on the **Search button**. A list of topics will appear.

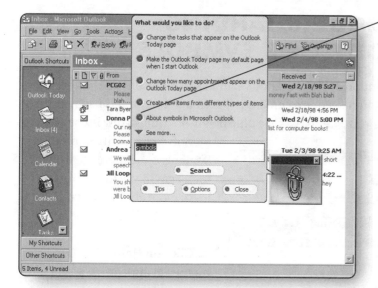

5. Click on **About symbols in Microsoft Outlook**. A Help window will open.

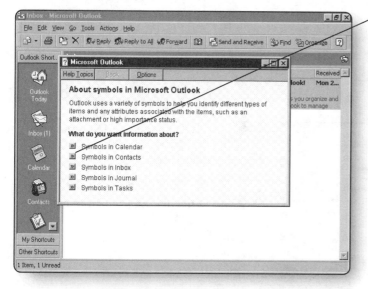

6. Click on any of the **topics** in the Microsoft Outlook window. The symbols used in Outlook will appear.

4 Getting the Help You Need

Outlook has so many features that you may need occasional assistance when you are first learning the program. Even after you learn to use Outlook, you'll find yourself checking the application's help often. Fortunately, Outlook gives you several ways to get help while working with the application. In this chapter, you'll learn how to:

✦ Use the Office Assistant

✦ Search Contents and Index

✦ Get help on the Web

USING THE OFFICE ASSISTANT

If you have used recent versions of Microsoft Office, you may already be familiar with the Office Assistant. The Office Assistant is a tool that provides an animated character that interacts with you to answer your questions about the application. The Office Assistant can be completely customized; in fact, you can even choose a different animated character (sometimes called an actor) for your Office Assistant if you don't like the current one.

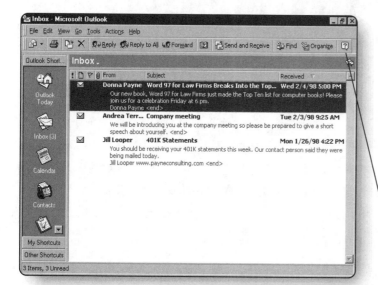

1. Click on the **Office Assistant button**. The Office Assistant will appear.

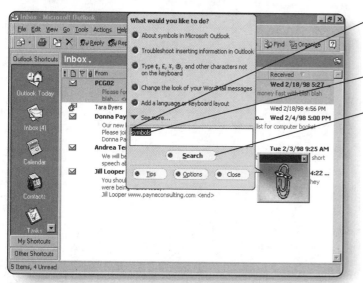

2. Click in the **text box**. The current text will be selected.

3. Type your **question**.

4. Click on **Search**. The Office Assistant will respond with a list of topics that match the words in your sentence to answer your question.

TIP

You can type natural language queries, such as "How do I print?" to find help on a specific topic. You do not need to type punctuation or proper capitalization in your help queries.

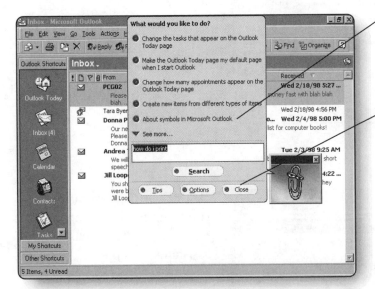

5. **Click** on any **topic** to get further help. A window will appear that expands on the topic you've selected.

6. **Click** on the **Close button** when you are finished. The window will close.

Selecting an Office Assistant

When you start Outlook, you will meet the default Office Assistant. If you get tired of this character, there are other assistants you can choose from if they were installed during your installation of Outlook. Each assistant has its own personality, so you can pick the assistant you learn from the best.

The Office Assistants are a shared component of the Microsoft Office 97 suite. If you would like to change your Office Assistant, and you do not have the Office 97 CD-ROM, you can download additional Office Assistant characters from Microsoft's Web site at http://www.microsoft.com.

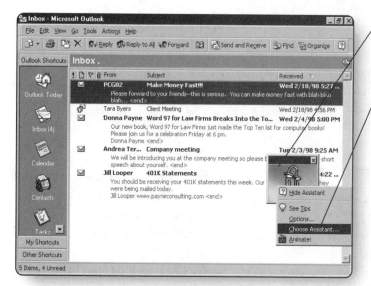

1. Right-click on **Office Assistant**. A shortcut menu will appear.

2. Click on **Choose Assistant**. The Office Assistant dialog box will open.

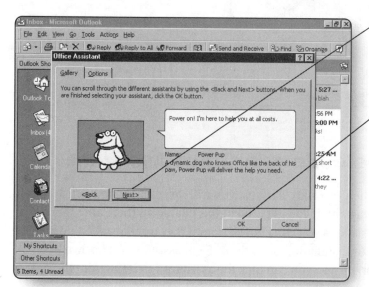

3. Click on the **Next button**. As you continue clicking on the Next button, the available assistants will appear.

4. Click on **OK**. The dialog box will close and your Office Assistant will change to the one you've selected.

Customizing the Office Assistant

As you work in Outlook, the Office Assistant will give you tips and suggestions to make your work easier. As you become more familiar with the application, you may need these tips less often. You can customize the Office Assistant so that it gives you only the information you need.

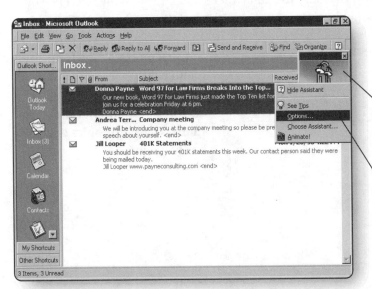

1. **Right-click** on **Office Assistant**. A shortcut menu will appear.

2. **Click** on **Options**. The Office Assistant dialog box will open.

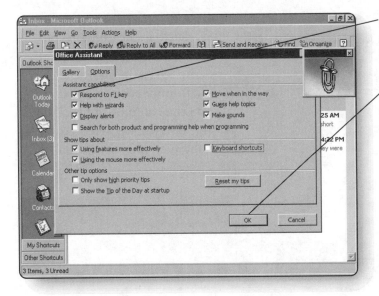

3. **Click** in the **check boxes** to select the options you want. The boxes will be checked.

4. **Click** on **OK**. The dialog box will close and your changes will be saved.

SEARCHING CONTENTS AND INDEX

Another way to get help is by using the online books provided with Outlook. You can either search through the reference by using the Index, or browse through the Table of Contents.

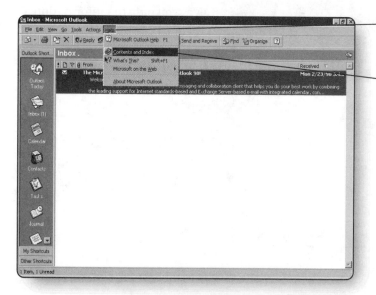

1. Click on **Help**. The Help menu will appear.

2. Click on **Contents and Index**. The Help Topics dialog box will open.

3. Click on the **Contents tab**. The tab will come to the front.

4. Double-click on any **topic**. You can continue until you find the item you want. If there are subtopics, more items will appear.

5. **Click** on the **Index tab**. The tab will come to the front.

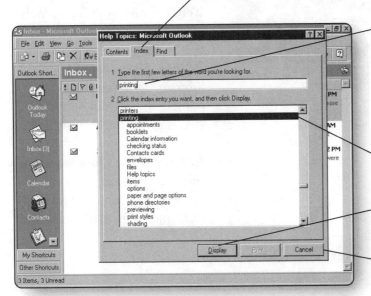

6. **Type** the first few letters of the **topic** for which you are searching in the first text box. The list will scroll to any words that begin with the letters you type.

7. **Click** on the **index entry** you want to view. It will be selected.

8. **Click** on **Display**. The corresponding help topic will appear.

9. **Click** on **Cancel** to close the window. The Help window will close.

GETTING HELP ON THE WEB

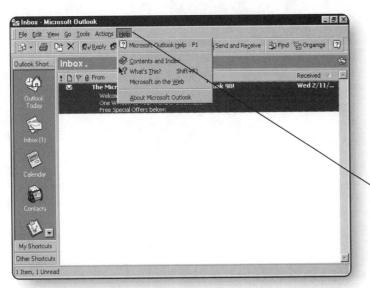

If you have access to the Internet, you can get help by using the World Wide Web and visiting Microsoft's Web site. Some topics available are frequently asked questions for Outlook, free stuff, and product news about Outlook.

1. **Click** on **Help**. The Help menu will appear.

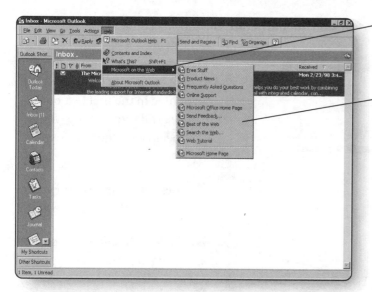

2. Click on **Microsoft on the Web**. The Microsoft on the Web submenu will appear.

3. Click on any **topic**. Your Web browser will appear and will point to the Outlook support Web site.

4. Click on the **Close button** in your Web browser when you are finished. Your Web browser will close and Outlook will reappear.

PART I REVIEW QUESTIONS

1. How do you start Outlook 98? *See "Starting Outlook" in Chapter 1*

2. How do you exit Outlook 98? *See "Exiting Outlook" in Chapter 1*

3. How do you access a menu command? *See "Using Menus" in Chapter 2*

4. Name two methods for closing a dialog box. *See "Exploring Dialog Boxes" in Chapter 2*

5. How do you view e-mail messages in the Information viewer? *See "Using the Outlook Bar" in Chapter 3*

6. Name two methods for displaying the folder list. *See "Displaying the Folder List" in Chapter 3*

7. What feature in Outlook 98 gives you a preview of your day? *See "Using Outlook Today" in Chapter 3*

8. What interactive feature in Outlook 98 provides answers to your questions? *See "Using Office Assistant" in Chapter 4*

9. Where can you search online reference manuals for Outlook 98? *See "Searching Contents and Index" in Chapter 4*

10. How can you get up-to-date help from Microsoft? *See "Getting Help on the Web" in Chapter 4*

PART II

Communicating with E-mail

nd:

1

ay

rsday

1998

anuary 1998

M T W T F S
29 30 31 1 2 3
5 6 7 8 9 10
11 12 13 14 15 16 17
18 19 20 21 22 23 24

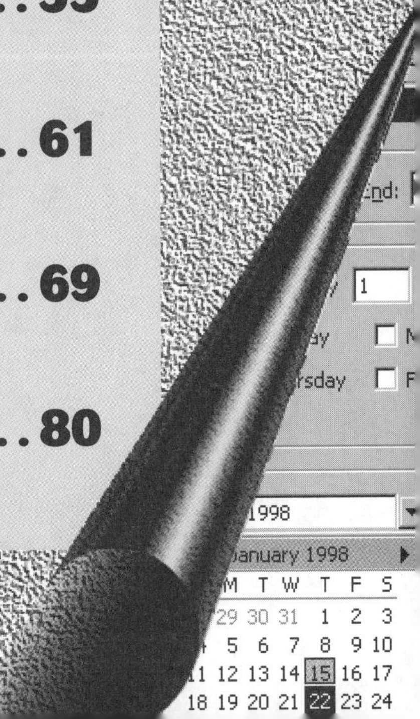

5 Creating New Messages

Ready to let the world know you're online? One of the first things you can do with Outlook is communicate with others via e-mail. Using e-mail is a fast and effective way to send messages to people. In Outlook, you can completely customize your e-mail messages, automatically add a signature, and even send documents along with e-mail. In this chapter, you'll learn how to:

+ Address an e-mail message

+ Format message text

+ Add an automatic signature

+ Check the spelling of a message

+ Set message options

+ Create draft messages

+ Attach a file

ADDRESSING AN E-MAIL MESSAGE

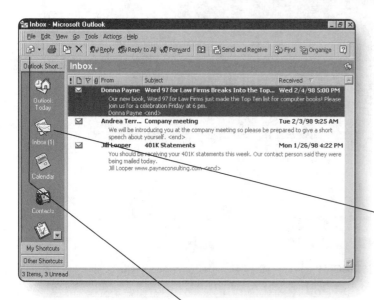

Every e-mail message must have an address so that Outlook knows how to deliver the message. An e-mail address can be a person's full name or some combination of their first and last name. Internet addresses have an @ symbol, such as president@whitehouse.gov.

1. **Click** on the **Inbox icon** on the Outlook bar. The Inbox contents will appear in the Information viewer.

2. **Click** on the **New Mail Message button**. A new message will appear.

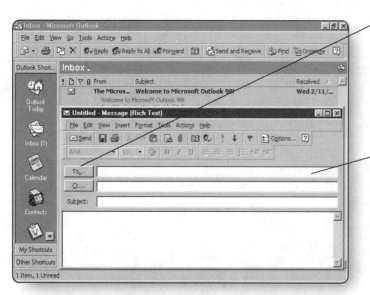

3. **Click** on the **To button** to access the Address Book. The Select Names dialog box will open.

NOTE

If you already know the e-mail address, you can type it directly in the To text box.

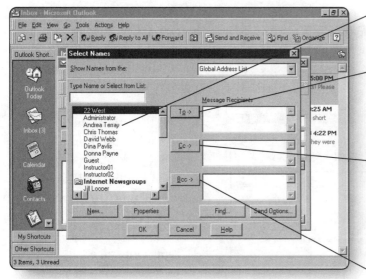

4. **Click** on a **name** from the list
of addresses.

5a. **Click** on the **To button**.
The message will be sent to the
selected individual.

OR

5b. **Click** on the **Cc button**.
A carbon copy of the message
will be sent to the selected
individual.

OR

5c. **Click** on the **Bcc button**.
A blind carbon copy of the
message will be sent to the
selected individual.

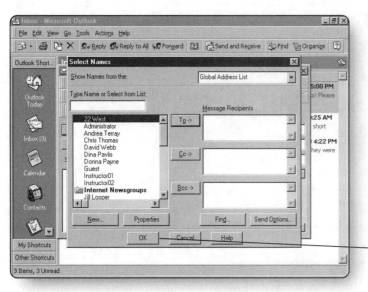

6. **Click** on **OK**. The Select
Names dialog box will close.

TIP

You can send the message to multiple people by separating their names with semicolons or commas in the To text box.

FORMATTING MESSAGE TEXT

You can type a message and send it immediately if you are pressed for time. However, if you have a few extra minutes, you can format your message so that the important points in the message stand out. Outlook has a Formatting toolbar with numerous options to change the look of your message.

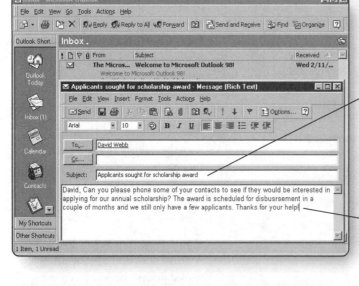

1. Type the **title of the message** in the Subject text box.

2. Press the **Tab key**. The cursor will move to the message text box.

3. Type a **message**.

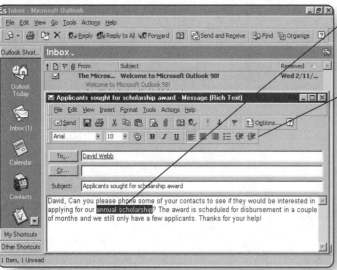

4. Click and drag the mouse over some text. The text will be selected.

5. Click on any **button** on the Formatting toolbar.

The options are:

✦ **Font**. Click on the down arrow (▼) to the right of the font name to select a different font.

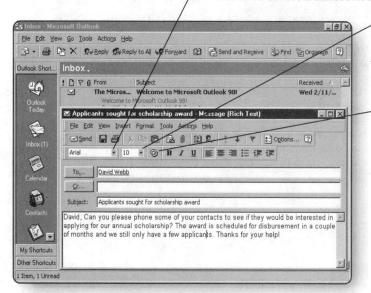

✦ **Font Size**. Click on the down arrow (▼) to the right of the font size to select a larger or smaller font size.

✦ **Font Color**. Click on the button to select a different font color.

✦ **Bold**. Click on the button to make the text bold.

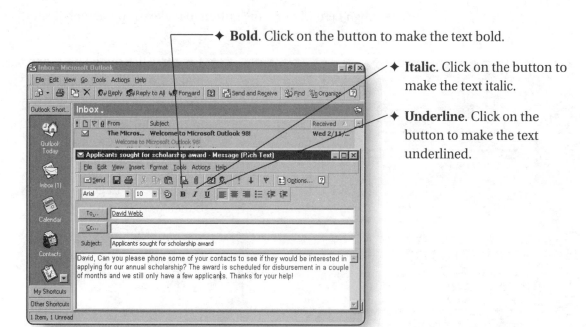

✦ **Italic**. Click on the button to make the text italic.

✦ **Underline**. Click on the button to make the text underlined.

Formatting Paragraphs

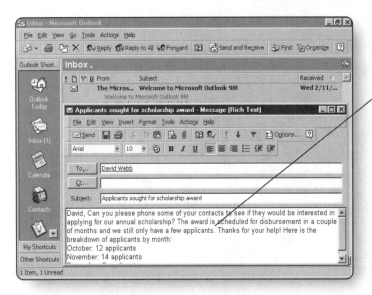

You can also format entire paragraphs by clicking buttons on the Formatting toolbar.

1a. **Click anywhere** in the paragraph you want to format.

OR

1b. **Click** and **drag** the mouse over several paragraphs to format more than one paragraph.

The paragraph formatting options are:

✦ **Align Left**. Click on the button to make the paragraph flush with the left margin.

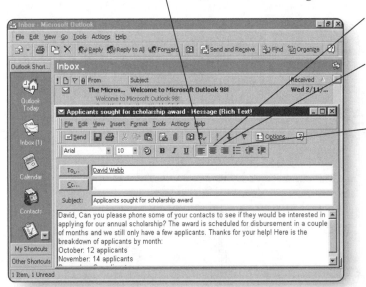

✦ **Center**. Click on the button to make the paragraph centered.

✦ **Align Right**. Click on the button to make the paragraph flush with the right margin.

✦ **Bullets**. Click on the button to make the paragraph bulleted.

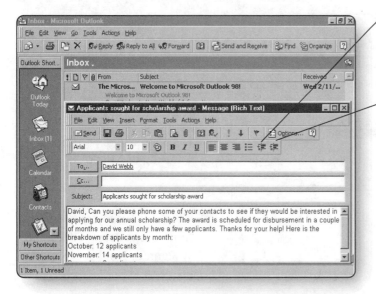

◆ **Decrease Indent**. Click on the button to decrease the indent of the paragraph from the left margin.

◆ **Increase Indent**. Click on the button to increase the indent from the left margin.

ADDING AN AUTOMATIC SIGNATURE

When you write a letter to someone, it's customary to add your signature to the bottom of the letter. E-mail is no different, but you have an advantage: Outlook can add your signature automatically so that you don't have to sign your e-mail each time.

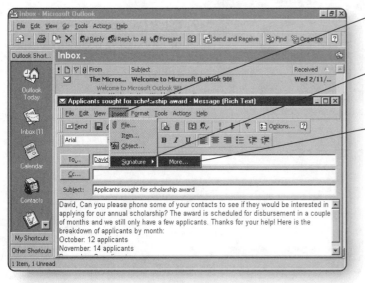

1. **Click** on **Insert**. The Insert menu will appear.

2. **Click** on **Signature**. The Signature submenu will appear.

3. **Click** on **More**.

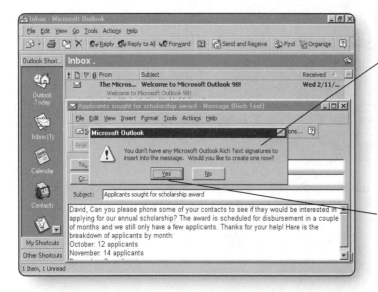

NOTE

If you have established a signature, a list of available signatures will appear. If you have not already established an automatic signature, a message will appear allowing you to do so.

4. **Click** on **Yes** to create an automatic signature. The Create New Signature dialog box will open.

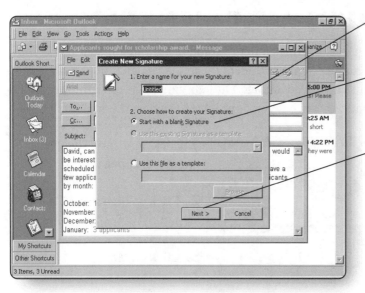

5. **Type** a **name** for the new signature in the first text box.

6. **Click** on **Start with a blank Signature**. The option button will be selected.

7. **Click** on **Next**. The Edit Signature dialog box will open.

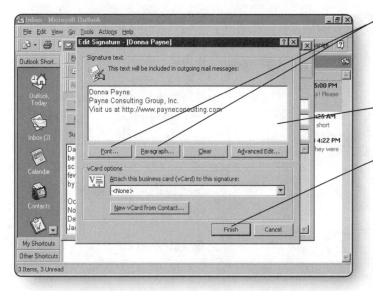

8. Click on the **Font button** or the **Paragraph button** to establish special formatting for the signature.

9. Type your **signature** in the text box.

10. Click on **Finish**. Your AutoSignature will be saved and the window will close.

11. Close the **message window**. If you are asked to save changes, click on no. The message window will disappear and you will return to the Inbox.

Choosing a Default Signature

You can create multiple signatures in Outlook. Whenever you need a signature in your e-mail message, you can click on Insert, Signature, and choose the signature you want. You can also choose a default signature that will automatically attach itself to any new, outgoing messages.

1. Click on **Tools**. The Tools menu will appear.

2. Click on **Options**. The Options dialog box will open.

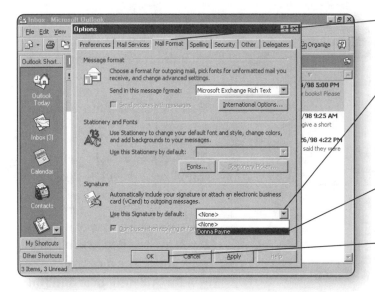

3. **Click** on the **Mail Format tab**. The tab will come to the front.

4. **Click** on the **down arrow** (▼) next to Use this Signature by default. A drop-down list will appear.

5. **Click** on the **signature** you want to use.

6. **Click** on **OK**. The Options dialog box will close.

CHECKING THE SPELLING OF A MESSAGE

Just because e-mail is fast doesn't mean it needs to be sloppy! Before sending your message, it's a good idea to check the spelling of the message.

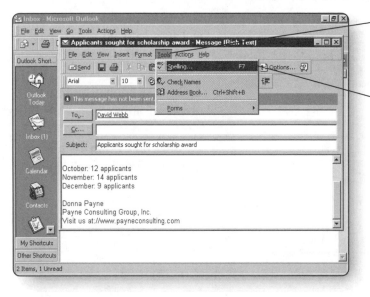

1. **Click** on **Tools** in the mail message. The Tools menu will appear.

2. **Click** on **Spelling**. The Spelling dialog box will open.

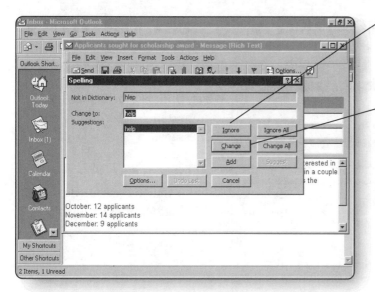

3a. Click on **Ignore** if you don't want to make the change.

OR

3b. Click on **Change** if you want to accept Outlook's proposed change.

4. Click on **Close** when you're finished spell-checking the document. The Spelling dialog box will close.

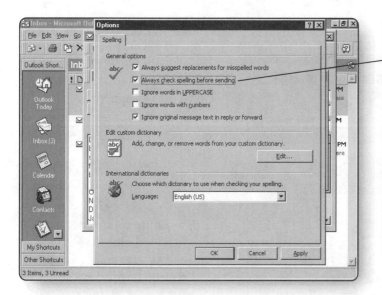

TIP

You can have Outlook automatically check the spelling before sending a message. While the Inbox is shown in the Information viewer, click on Tools, Options, and then select the Spelling tab. Click on the check box next to Always check spelling before sending and then click on OK.

SETTING MESSAGE OPTIONS

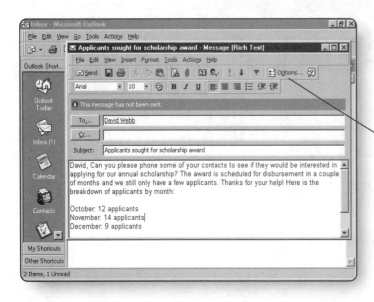

Before you send the message, there are many options you can set. Options can change the importance or sensitivity of a message.

1. **Click** on the **Options button** in the mail message. The Message Options dialog box will open.

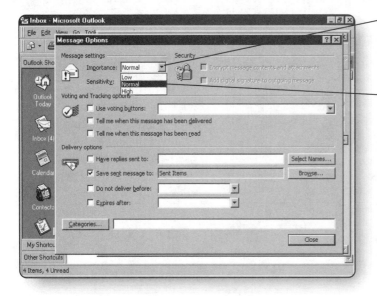

2. **Click** on the **down arrow** (▼) next to Importance. A drop-down list will appear.

3. **Click** on **Normal**, **Low**, or **High**.

NOTE

A low importance message will have a blue down-pointing arrow, and a high importance message will have a red exclamation point when delivered.

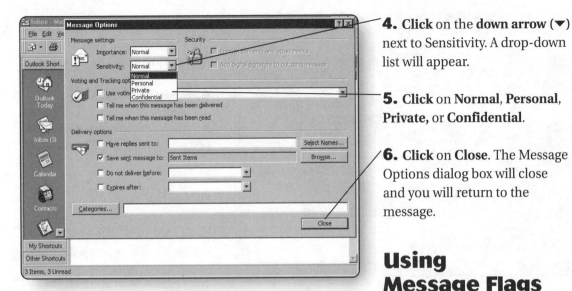

4. Click on the **down arrow (▼)** next to Sensitivity. A drop-down list will appear.

5. Click on **Normal**, **Personal**, **Private,** or **Confidential**.

6. Click on **Close**. The Message Options dialog box will close and you will return to the message.

Using Message Flags

You can add a message flag to an e-mail message. Message flags add notes to the message recipients, letting them know that a follow up is due by a certain date, or that no follow up is necessary.

NOTE

Personal, Private, and Confidential messages will have a banner just below the To line at the top of the e-mail message with a note saying "Please treat this message as Personal" (or Confidential). Also, once you send a private message, the recipient will not be able to modify the contents.

1. Click on **Actions** in the mail message. The Actions menu will appear.

2. Click on **Flag for Follow Up**. The Flag for Follow Up dialog box will open.

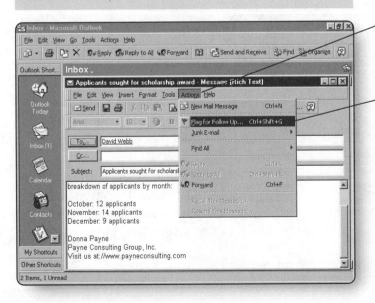

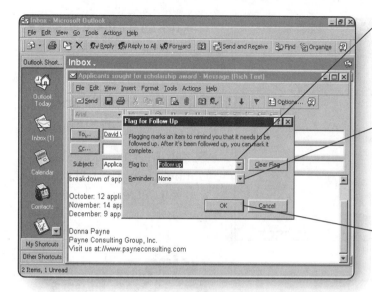

3. **Click** on the **down arrow (▼)** to the right of the Flag to list box. A drop-down list will appear.

4. **Select** a **message flag**.

5. **Click** on the **down arrow** (▼) to the right of the Reminder list box.

6. **Select** a **date**.

7. **Click** on **OK**. The Flag for Follow Up dialog box will close and you will return to the message.

CREATING A DRAFT MESSAGE

If you are composing a long e-mail and decide to finish it later, you can save the message as a draft.

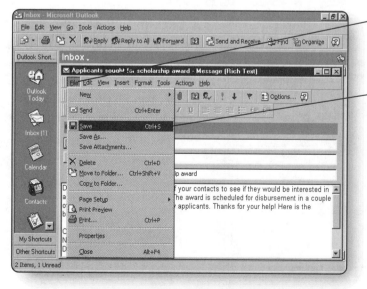

1. **Click** on **File** on an unsent message. The File menu will appear.

2. **Click** on **Save**. The message will be copied to the Drafts folder.

3. **Click** on **Close**. The message will close and be saved in the Drafts folder. You can finish it when you have more time.

Working with Draft Messages

1. **Click** on the **My Shortcuts group** on the Outlook bar. The My Shortcuts group will be revealed on the Outlook bar.

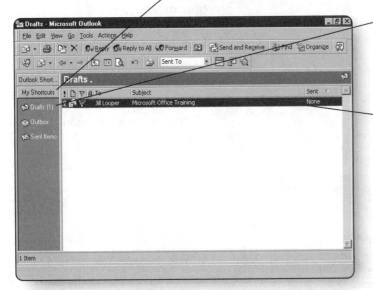

2. **Click** on the **Drafts icon**. The contents of the Drafts folder will appear in the Information viewer.

3. **Double-click** on the **draft message** in the Information viewer. The draft message will open. Once the message is open, you can continue working on the text until you are ready to send the message.

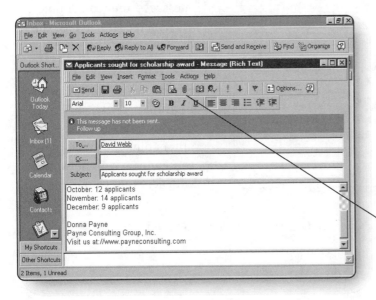

ATTACHING A FILE

Before you send a message, you may need to attach a file (document) to the e-mail message. Outlook gives you an easy way to attach files to e-mail messages.

1. **Click** on the **Insert File button**. The Insert File dialog box will open.

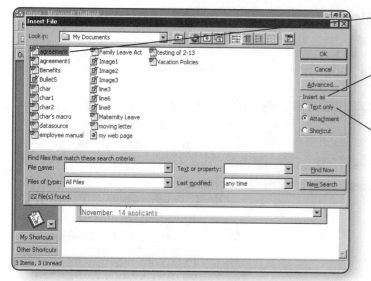

2. Click on the **file** you want to attach. It will be selected.

3. Click on an **Insert as option button**. They are:

✦ **Text only**. The file will be inserted as text in the body of the e-mail message. It's sometimes a good idea to use this option when sending files via the Internet.

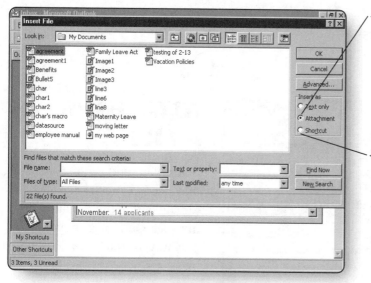

✦ **Attachment**. The file will be inserted as an icon in the body of the message. When recipients receive e-mail messages, they can double-click on the icon to read the attachment.

✦ **Shortcut**. A shortcut to the file will be inserted in the body of the message. Do not use this method unless you are sending the message to someone on your network or with access to your computer.

4. Click on **OK**. The file will be attached.

6 Sending Mail

Once you have finished composing your e-mail message and setting options, it's a snap to send the message. Outlook will also allow you to view your sent messages and resend or forward them as many times as you like. In this chapter, you'll learn how to:

✦ Send a mail message

✦ View messages in the Sent Items folder

✦ Recall a message

✦ Resend a message

SENDING A MAIL MESSAGE

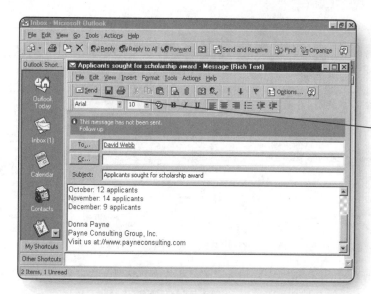

You've written the message, addressed it to the appropriate people, and set all of the available options. Now all that's left to do is send the message.

1. **Click** on the **Send button**. The message will be sent.

VIEWING AND SORTING SENT MESSAGES

Trying to remember if you sent a message to someone can be tricky. Luckily, Outlook allows you to view all of the messages you have sent, and it helps keep your messages organized.

NOTE

When you send a message, it temporarily moves to the Outbox. Once the message has been sent, it moves to the Sent Items folder.

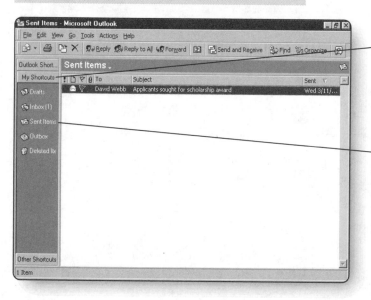

1. **Click** on the **My Shortcuts button** on the Outlook bar. The contents of the My Shortcuts folder will appear in the Information viewer.

2. **Click** on the **Sent Items icon** on the Outlook bar. The contents of the Sent Items folder will appear in the Information viewer.

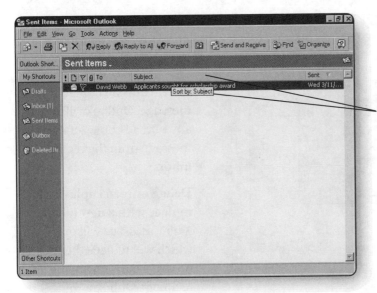

You can sort messages in the Sent Items folder to quickly locate the message for which you are looking.

3. Click on any **column header**. The messages will be sorted by that field.

RECALLING A MESSAGE

Ever had a sinking feeling as soon as you pressed the Send button? "I wish I hadn't sent that e-mail!" Outlook gives you a safety net with the Recall feature. Recall is also a good feature to use when you discover incorrect information in the message you have sent.

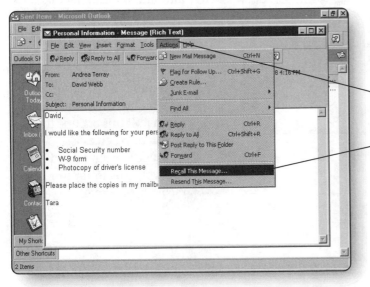

1. Click twice on a **message** in the Sent Items folder. The message will open.

2. Click on **Actions**. The Actions menu will appear.

3. Click on **Recall This Message**. The Recall This Message dialog box will open.

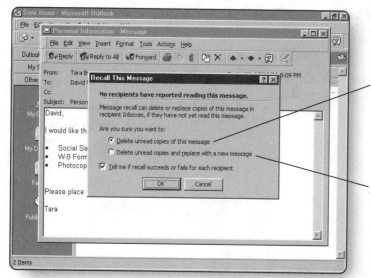

There are several options available when recalling a message. They are:

✦ **Delete unread copies of this message**. Outlook will delete any unread copies of the message from the recipient's Inbox.

✦ **Delete unread copies and replace with a new message**. A new message will open, which will replace the message currently in the recipient's Inbox.

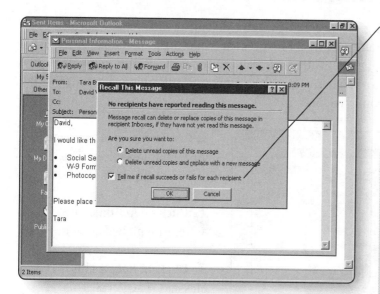

✦ **Tell me if recall succeeds or fails for each recipient**. Outlook sends you a new e-mail message informing you of success or failure of the attempt to recall the message.

NOTE

Recall failure occurs if the recipient has read the message before you attempt to recall it. If this occurs, the recipient receives a message warning them that you are attempting to recall the original message.

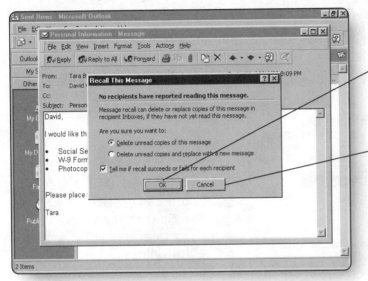

4. **Click** on the **options** you want to use.

5a. **Click** on **OK**. The message will be recalled.

OR

5b. **Click** on **Cancel**. The message recall will be canceled.

RESENDING A MESSAGE

Sometimes message recipients may tell you that they didn't receive your message. Or you may send a message and then realize that you forgot to include an important recipient. Resending the message allows you to quickly handle both situations.

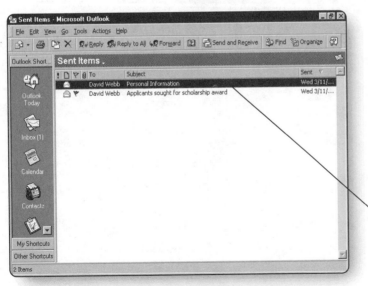

Also if you are tired of typing the same messages week after week (for example, an e-mail message to the office asking for lunch orders, or a weekly status report), resending a message can save you valuable time. Messages can be edited before they are resent.

1. **Click twice** on the **message** in the Sent Items folder. The message will open.

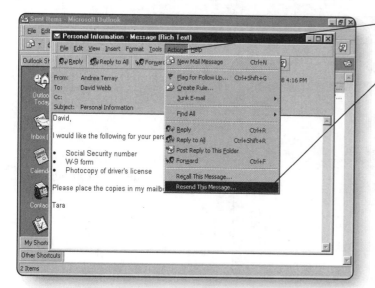

2. Click on **Actions**. The Actions menu will appear.

3. Click on **Resend This Message**. The message will open as a new e-mail message.

TIP

You can edit the message text, add or delete message recipients, and change message options before resending.

4. Click on the **Send button**. The message will be sent again.

NOTE

Resending a message will not remove the original message from the recipient's Inbox. You must recall a message to delete the original message.

7 Keeping Track of Messages

After you have sent many e-mail messages, you may feel overwhelmed by the number of items in the Sent Items folder. Don't worry, Outlook gives you several ways to keep track of your messages by setting message options. In this chapter, you'll learn how to:

◆ Receive notification when a message is read

◆ Send replies to another individual

◆ Deliver a message at a specific time

◆ Expire a message

NOTE
You must set the option to receive notification *before* the message is sent.

RECEIVING NOTIFICATION WHEN A MESSAGE IS READ

Say you've sent an important e-mail message to someone and you want to follow up with a phone call. How do you know when they have read the message? It's easy! All you have

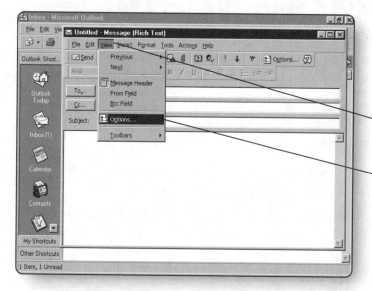

to do is tell Outlook to notify you when the message has been read.

1. Create a **new mail message**.

2. **Click** on **View**. The View menu will appear.

3. **Click** on **Options**. The Message Options dialog box will open.

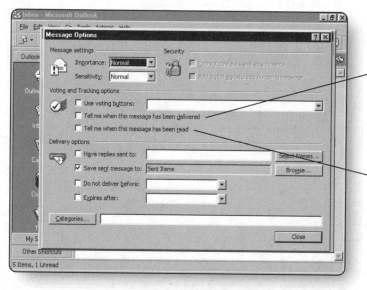

There are two notification options:

✦ **Tell me when this message has been delivered**. Outlook will notify you when the message has reached the recipient's Inbox.

✦ **Tell me when this message has been read**. Outlook will notify you when the message has been opened.

NOTE

If the message is sent to someone outside of your company via the Internet, Outlook will only be able to tell you when the message has been delivered, not when it has been read.

TIP

If you use tracking options frequently, you can set all of your new messages to automatically have tracking. In the Inbox, click on Tools, Options, and click on the E-mail Options button. When the E-mail Options dialog box opens, click on the Tracking Options button and select the tracking options you want to use.

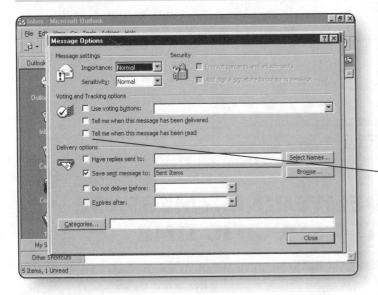

4. Click on the **check box(es)** of one or both of the tracking options. The option(s) will be selected.

SENDING REPLIES TO ANOTHER INDIVIDUAL

Normally, when people reply to an e-mail message, the reply is sent back to the message sender. However, you can have replies sent directly to another individual.

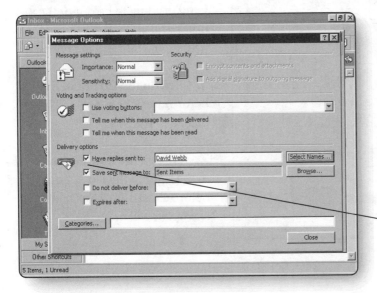

1. Click on the **Have Replies Sent to check box**. A ✔ will be placed in the box.

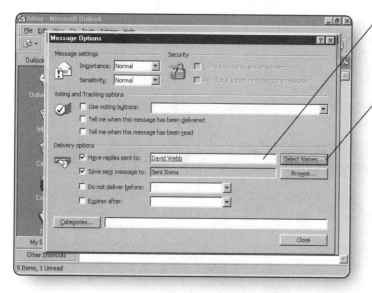

2a. Type the individual's e-mail address in the text box.

OR

2b. Click on the Select Names button and select the individual's name from the address book.

DELIVERING A MESSAGE AT A SPECIFIC TIME

Messages are normally delivered as soon as you send them. However, you can delay the delivery of a message to a specific time. This feature works great if you are going to be out of the office and still want an e-mail delivered while you are gone.

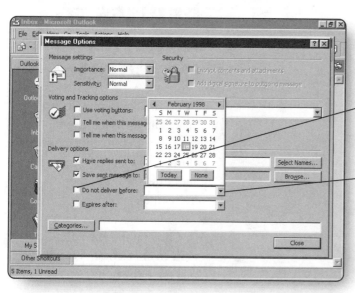

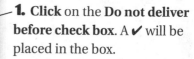

1. Click on the **Do not deliver before check box**. A ✔ will be placed in the box.

2. Click on the **down arrow** (▼) to the right of the Do not deliver before check box. The Date Navigator will open.

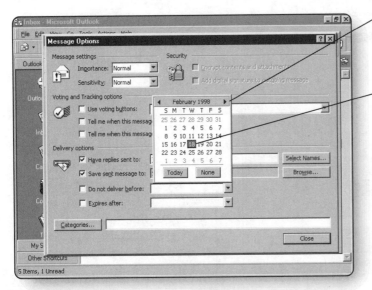

3. Click on the **left** or **right arrow** on either side of the month. The month will change.

4. Click on the **date** you want when the correct month is displayed.

TIP

You can type a different date or time directly into the Do not deliver before text box.

NOTE

The message will remain in your Outbox until the specified delivery time. You can edit the message or delete the message from the Outbox.

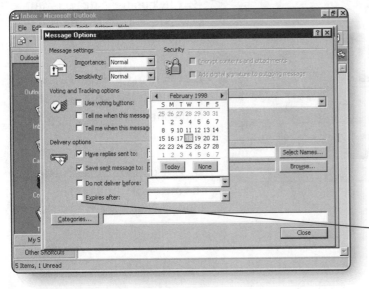

EXPIRING A MESSAGE

Have you ever been out of the office and returned to find a ton of out-of-date e-mail messages in your Inbox? It's considered good e-mail manners to expire your messages if they contain time-sensitive material.

1. Click on the **Expires after check box**. A ✔ will be placed in the box.

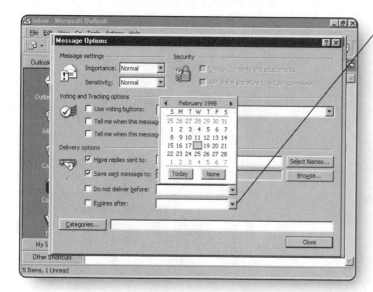

2. Click on the **down arrow (▼)** to the right of the Expires after check box. The Date Navigator will open.

NOTE

Expired messages remain in the recipient's Inbox, but they are highlighted with strikethrough formatting for easy identification.

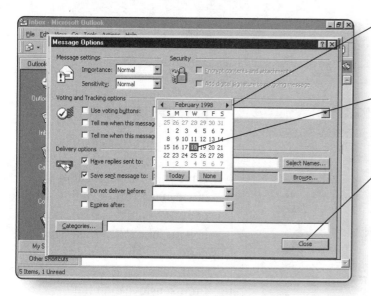

3. Click on the **left** or **right arrow** on either side of the month. The month will change.

4. Click on the **date** you want when the correct month is displayed.

5. Click on **Close**. The Message Options dialog box will close and your unsent message will reappear.

6. Click on the **Close button** in the message window. The message will close.

8 Working with E-mail Messages

You'll probably use e-mail more than any other feature in Outlook. Sending and receiving e-mail is now an integral part of doing business and communicating with others. Once you receive e-mail, you'll need to know what to do with it. In this chapter, you'll learn how to:

✦ Change how you view e-mail messages

✦ Use AutoPreview or the Preview Pane

✦ Read, reply, forward, delete, and print a message

✦ Navigate between e-mail messages

CHANGING HOW YOU VIEW YOUR E-MAIL MESSAGES

Views in Outlook provide you with different ways to look at information in a folder by putting it in different arrangements and formats. Use views to control how much detail appears in your e-mail messages.

1. **Click** on the **Inbox icon** on the Outlook bar. The Inbox contents will appear in the Information viewer.

2. **Click** on **View**. The View menu will appear.

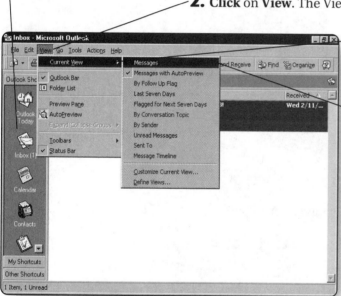

3. **Click** on **Current View**. The Current View submenu will appear.

4. **Click** on any **View**. Your e-mail messages will appear differently in the Information viewer.

TIP

If you find a view that is close to what you are looking for, you can click on View, Current View, and Customize Current View. From there, you can specify exactly how you want your e-mail messages to appear.

Using AutoPreview

AutoPreview is a way to quickly view the first three lines of an e-mail message without opening the message. Using AutoPreview saves you time and lets you open only the messages you want to read.

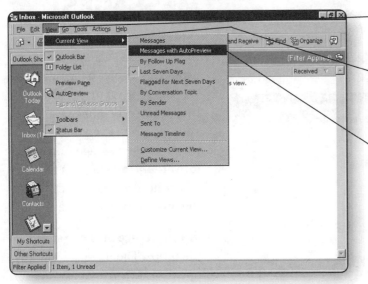

1. Click on **View**. The View menu will appear.

2. Click on **Current View**. The Current View submenu will appear.

3. Click on **Messages with AutoPreview**. Your Inbox will display up to the first three lines of e-mail messages you've received but have not yet read.

Using the Preview Pane

Another feature that lets you see a snapshot of your e-mail message is the Preview Pane. The Preview Pane divides the Information viewer in half: you can see the message header on the top half of the screen and the actual message on the bottom half of the screen.

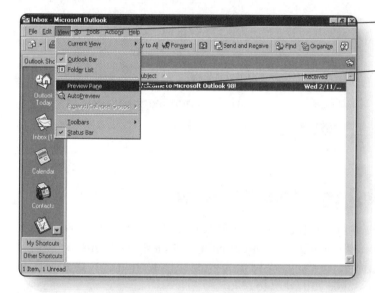

1. Click on **View**. The View menu will appear.

2. Click on **Preview Pane**. Your Information viewer will split, showing your regular Inbox view above and the body of the selected message below.

3. Click on **Preview Pane** again. It will turn off.

RESPONDING TO E-MAIL MESSAGES

One great thing about e-mail is that there are so many options when you receive a message. You can reply to the sender of the message, or you can send your replies to everyone who received the message. You can forward the message on to someone else, and you can print the message for your files.

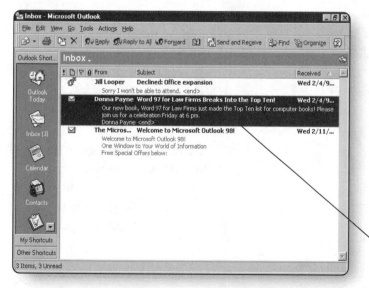

1. Click twice on a **message** in the Inbox. The message will open.

Choose one of the **following options**:

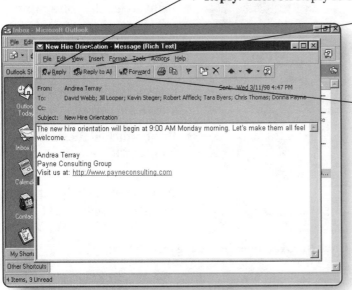

✦ **Reply**. Click on Reply to send a reply to the message sender.

✦ **Reply to All**. Click on Reply to All to send a reply to the message sender and all of the message recipients.

✦ **Forward**. Click on Forward to send the message to another person.

2. Type the **message text**.

3. Click on **Send**. Your message will be sent.

PRINTING A MESSAGE

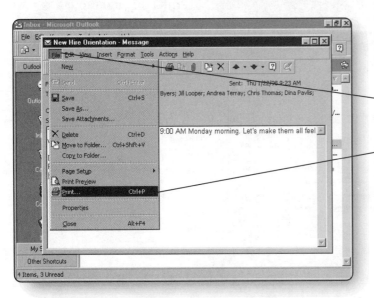

You can keep e-mail messages in your Inbox, or you can print messages for future reference.

1. Click on **File**. The File menu will appear.

2. Click on **Print**. The Print dialog box will open.

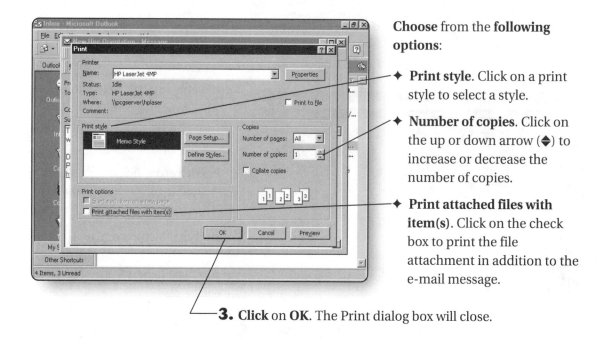

Choose from the **following options**:

✦ **Print style**. Click on a print style to select a style.

✦ **Number of copies**. Click on the up or down arrow (✦) to increase or decrease the number of copies.

✦ **Print attached files with item(s)**. Click on the check box to print the file attachment in addition to the e-mail message.

3. **Click** on **OK**. The Print dialog box will close.

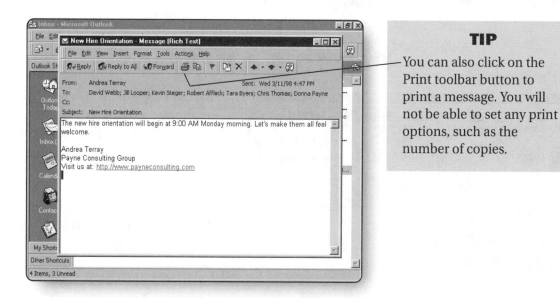

TIP

You can also click on the Print toolbar button to print a message. You will not be able to set any print options, such as the number of copies.

NAVIGATING BETWEEN E-MAIL MESSAGES

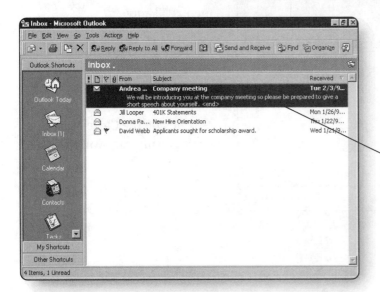

After a while, you will have numerous messages in your Inbox. Learning how to move around will help you locate the messages you want more quickly.

1. **Click twice** on any **message** in the Inbox. The message will open.

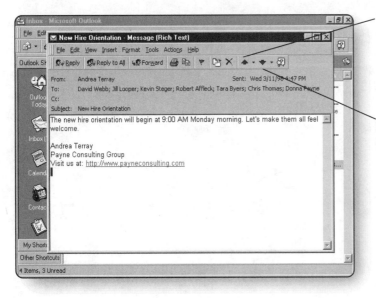

2a. **Click** on the **Previous Item button**. You will move to the previous e-mail message.

OR

2b. **Click** on the **Next Item button**. You will move to the next e-mail message.

There are down arrows (▼) to the right of the Next and Previous Item buttons. These give you more options so you can go to the next or previous item of a specific type.

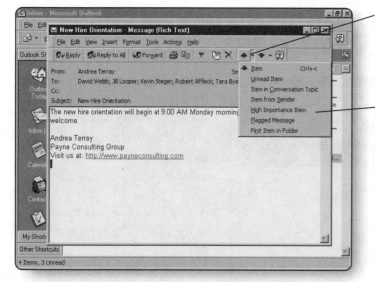

3. **Click** on the **down arrow** (▼) next to the Previous Item or Next Item buttons. A drop-down menu will appear.

4. **Click** on a **type**. You will move to the next or previous item of that type.

5. **Click** on the **Close button** (⊠). The message will close.

9 Using the Address Book

Many e-mail addresses are long and filled with special symbols or characters. Outlook has an address book to keep all of your e-mail addresses handy. This reduces the chance of mistyping an address, which could send your e-mail message to the wrong person or cause a delay in delivery. In this chapter, you'll learn how to:

✦ Add new addresses

✦ Use the Contacts folder as your address book

✦ Use Personal Distribution Lists

✦ Edit Personal Distribution Lists

✦ Delete Address Book entries

CREATING NEW E-MAIL ADDRESSES

If you are sending an e-mail message to some people and think that you may need to write to them again, it's a good idea to add the addresses to your address book. If you work for a company, many e-mail addresses may already be stored in the Global Address List. In this section, you will learn how to add an address to your Personal Address Book.

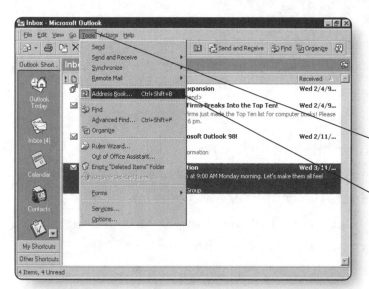

1. Click on **Tools**. The Tools menu will appear.

2. Click on **Address Book**. The Address Book window will appear.

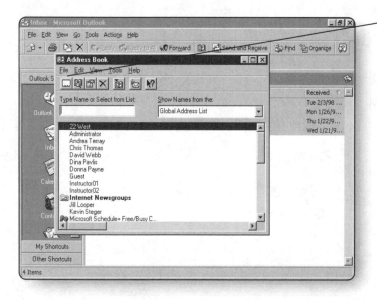

3. Click on the **New Entry button**. The New Entry dialog box will open.

4. **Click** on **Other Address** in the Select the entry type list box.

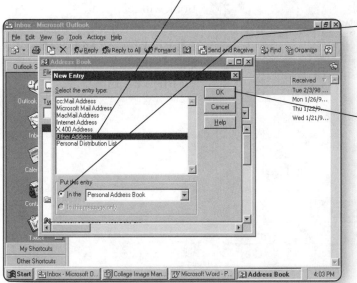

5. **Click** on **Personal Address Book** in the Put this entry section of the New Entry dialog box. The option will be selected.

6. **Click** on **OK**. The New Other Address Properties dialog box will open.

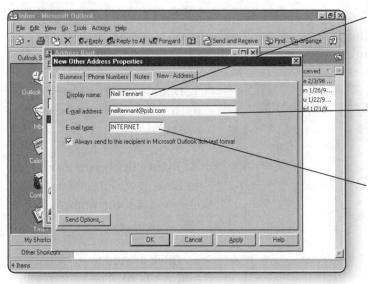

7. **Type** the person's **name** as you would like it to appear in the address book in the Display name text box.

8. **Type** the person's **e-mail address** in the E-mail address text box.

9. **Type** the **e-mail type** in the E-mail type text box.

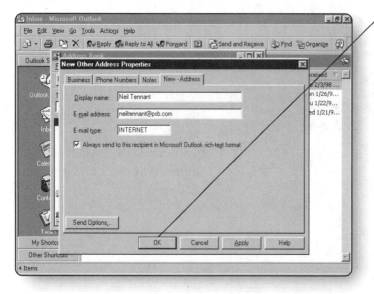

10. **Click** on **OK**. The Address Book will reappear.

11. **Click** on the **Address Book Close button** (⊠). You will return to the Inbox.

Using Addresses from Messages You Have Received

If you receive an e-mail message from someone, Outlook automatically knows the person's e-mail address. It's quick and easy for you to add the address to your address book.

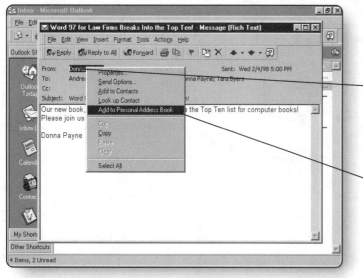

1. **Double-click** on a **message** in the Inbox. The e-mail message will open.

2. **Right-click** on the **e-mail address** in the From line of the message. A shortcut menu will appear.

3. **Click** on **Add to Personal Address Book**. The address will be stored in your Personal Address Book.

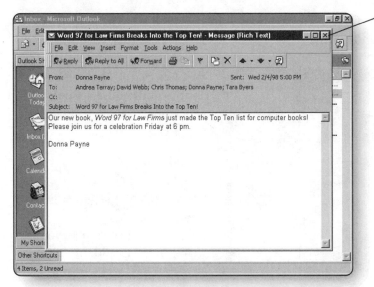

4. Click on the **Close button** ([X]). The message will close and you will return to the Inbox.

USING THE CONTACTS FOLDER AS AN ADDRESS BOOK

Outlook has several options for storing e-mail addresses. They can be kept in the Address Book, as shown previously, or they can be stored in the Contacts folder. You'll learn more about contacts in Chapter 16. Right now, you can set up the Contacts folder so it can be used when addressing e-mail messages.

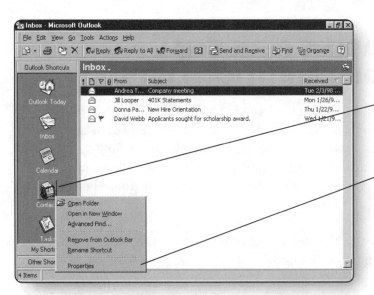

1. Right-click on the **Contacts icon** in the Outlook bar. A shortcut menu will appear.

2. Click on **Properties**. The Contacts Properties dialog box will open.

3. **Click** on the **Outlook Address Book tab**. The tab will come to the front.

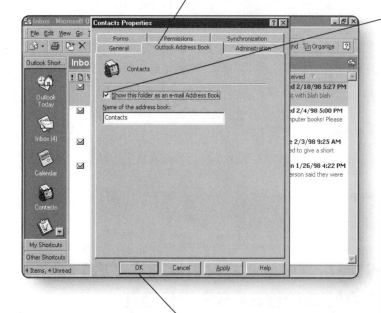

4. **Click** on the **Show this folder as an e-mail Address Book check box**. A ✔ will be placed in the box.

NOTE

If the Show this folder as an e-mail Address Book check box appears dimmed, you may need to add the Outlook Address Book as a service. Click on Tools, Services, and then click on the Add button. Select Outlook Address Book and click on OK.

5. **Click** on **OK**. You will have an address book called Contacts, where you can store e-mail addresses.

USING PERSONAL DISTRIBUTION LISTS

You know that you can send a message to multiple people by typing their names in the To box. If you send messages to the same group of people on a regular basis, creating an e-mail group will save you time and will guarantee that you don't forget anyone. Outlook calls these e-mail groups Personal Distribution Lists (PDLs).

1. **Click** on the **Address Book button**. The Address Book window will appear.

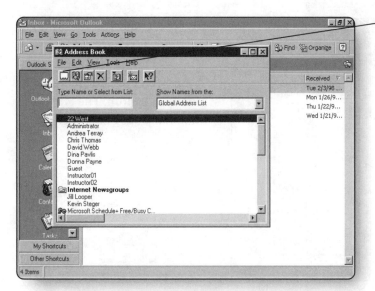

2. Click on the **New Entry button** in the Address Book. The New Entry dialog box will open.

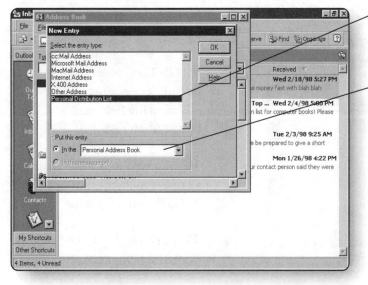

3. Click on **Personal Distribution List** in the Select the entry type list box.

4. Click on **Personal Address Book** in the Put this entry section of the New Entry dialog box. The option will be selected.

5. Click on **OK**. The New Other Personal Distribution List Properties dialog box will open.

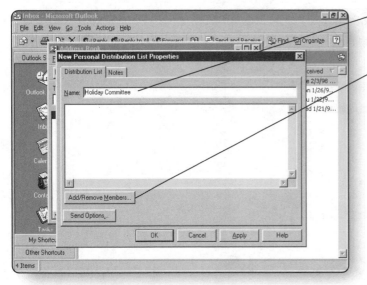

6. Type a **name** for the group in the Name text box.

7. Click on the **Add/Remove Members button**. The Edit Members dialog box will open.

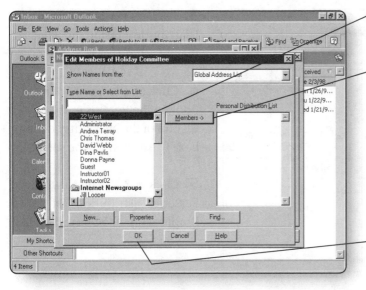

8. Click on an **address**. It will be selected.

9. Click on the **Members button**. The address will be added to the Personal Distribution List.

10. Repeat steps **8** and **9** until all of the members are included in the Personal Distribution List.

11. Click on **OK**. The Address Book will reappear.

EDITING E-MAIL GROUPS

When you store your Personal Distribution Lists in the Personal Address Book, it is your responsibility to keep them up-to-date. For example, if you have a list with members of a committee, you will need to edit the list as new members join the committee and other members leave the committee.

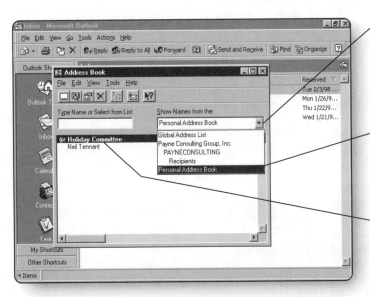

1. **Click** on the **down arrow (▼)** to the right of the Show Names from the list box in the Address Book. A drop-down list will appear.

2. **Click** on **Personal Address Book**. The contents of your Personal Address Book will appear in the box below.

3. **Click twice** on the **Personal Distribution List** in the list of entries. The Properties dialog box will open.

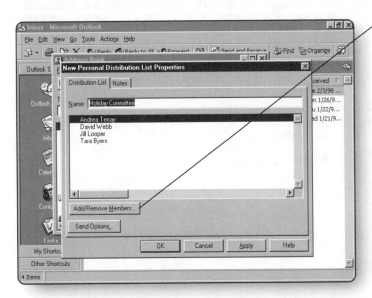

4. **Click** on the **Add/Remove Members button** to edit the list. The Edit Members dialog box will open.

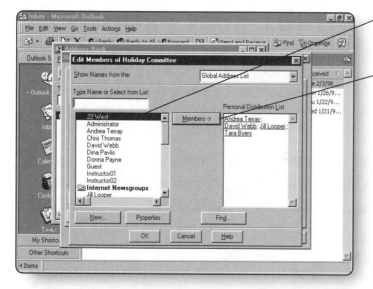

5. Click on a **name**. It will be selected.

6. Click on the **Members button**. The person will be added to the list.

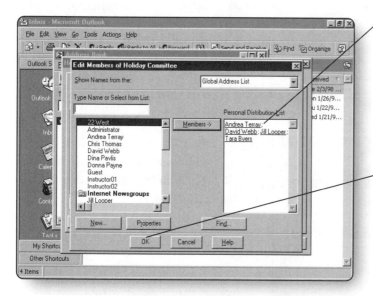

7. Click on a **name** in the Personal Distribution List. It will be selected.

8. Press the **Delete key**. The person will be removed from the list.

9. Click on **OK**. The Address Book will reappear.

DELETING ADDRESS BOOK ENTRIES

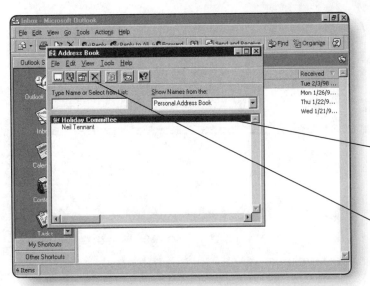

You may create an e-mail group for a project and no longer need the group when the project is complete. It's easy to delete entries from the Personal Address Book.

1. **Click** on the **entry** in the Address Book you want to delete. It will be selected.

2. **Click** on the **Delete button**. A confirmation message will appear.

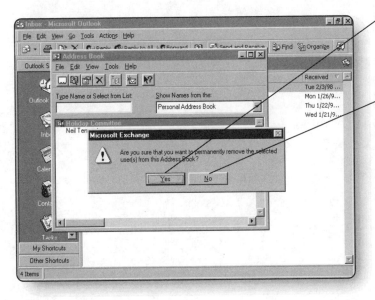

3a. **Click** on **Yes**. The entry will be permanently deleted.

OR

3b. **Click** on **No**. The deletion will be canceled.

10 Managing Your Messages

You know how easy it is to let piles of paper stack up on your desk! Outlook gives you many tools to organize your messages so your Inbox remains uncluttered and you can easily locate the messages you need. In this chapter, you'll learn how to:

✦ Organize messages in folders

✦ Organize messages with color

✦ Control junk and adult-content mail

✦ Use the Rules Wizard

✦ Find, sort, and archive messages

ORGANIZING MESSAGES IN FOLDERS

Think of your Inbox as a drawer in a filing cabinet. Would you just toss all of the messages into the drawer? No! You may read some mail immediately and throw it away, or you may need to store some messages while you wait for more information. Using electronic folders is an easy way to organize all of your messages, just as you would use file folders in a filing cabinet. Outlook lets you create new folders in your Inbox and move messages into the folders manually or automatically.

1. **Click** on the **Inbox icon** on the Outlook bar.

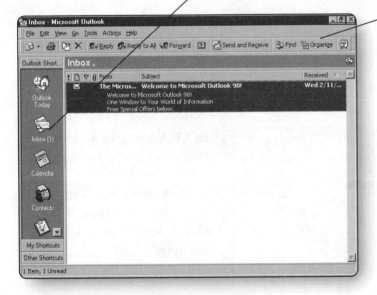

2. **Click** on the **Organize button**. The Ways to Organize Inbox pane will appear in the Information viewer.

3. **Click** on **Using Folders**. The Using Folders pane will come to the front.

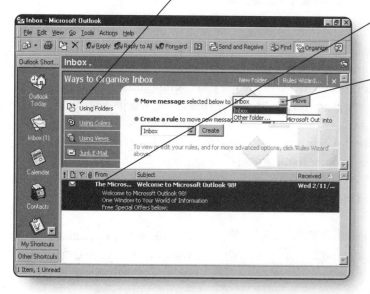

4. **Click** on the **message** you want to place in a folder.

5. **Click** on the **down arrow (▼)** to the right of Move message selected below. If your Inbox has folders, a list will appear. Otherwise, the Select Folder dialog box will open.

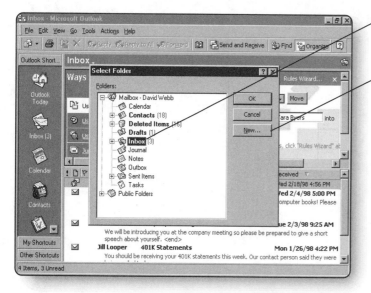

6. **Click** on the **folder** in which you want to store the message.

7. **Click** on the **New button** if the folder does not exist. The Create New Folder dialog box will open.

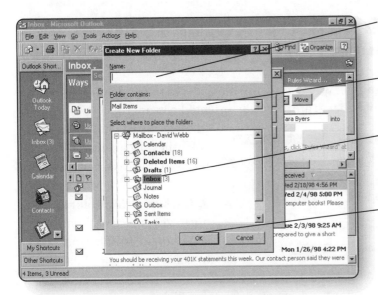

8. **Type** the **name** of the new folder in the Name text box.

9. **Click** on **Mail Items** in the Folder contains list box.

10. **Click** on **Inbox** to make the new folder a subfolder of the Inbox.

11. **Click** on **OK**. The message will be moved to the new subfolder.

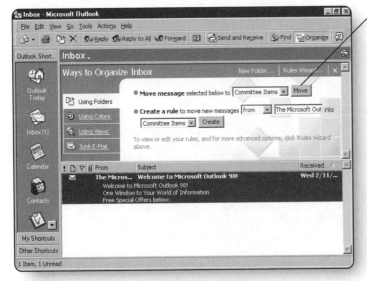

12. **Click** on the **Move button**. The selected message will be moved to the folder.

TIP

You can move multiple messages into a folder at once. When selecting the messages from the list of items in the Inbox, hold down the Shift key while you click on the messages.

ORGANIZING MESSAGES WITH COLOR

Another way to organize messages in the Inbox is by using color. If you are a visually-oriented person, you'll appreciate this feature of Outlook. You can color messages sent to or received from a certain person.

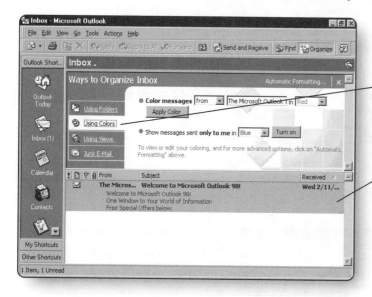

1. Click on **Using Colors**. Your organizer pane will change to allow you to organize messages by color.

2. Click on a **message** you want to color.

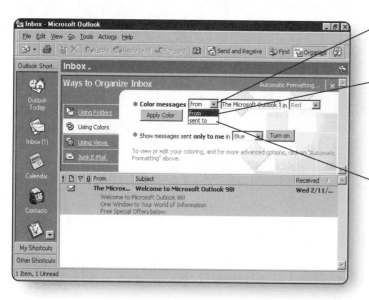

3. Click on the **down arrow (▼)** to the right of Color messages.

4a. Click on **from** to color messages from the selected individual.

OR

4b. Click on **sent to** to color messages sent to the selected individual.

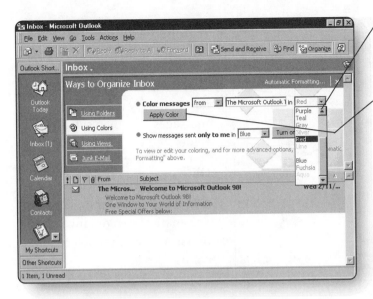

5. Click on the **down arrow** (▼) to the right of the color and select a color.

6. Click on the **Apply Color button**. Messages received from or sent to the individual you've selected will now be color-coded.

CONTROLLING JUNK AND ADULT-CONTENT MAIL

Ever heard of "spamming"? This is a term used to describe unsolicited e-mail that arrives in your Inbox. Unfortunately, once your e-mail address becomes public, you may receive junk mail in your Inbox frequently. Luckily, Outlook has created a special feature to control the junk and adult-content mail you receive. You can automatically color, move, or delete any junk or adult-content e-mail.

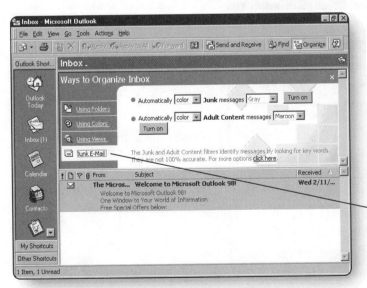

1. Click on **Junk E-Mail**. Your organizer pane will change to allow you to control undesirable messages.

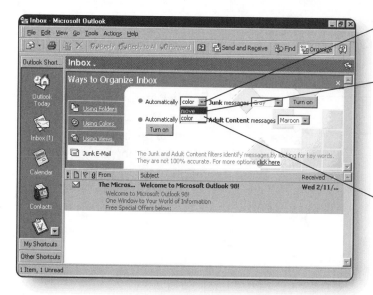

2. **Click** on the **down arrow** (▼) to the right of Automatically.

3a. **Click** on **move** to automatically move junk messages, and then **select** a **folder**.

OR

3b. **Click** on **color** to automatically color junk messages, and then **select** a **color**.

NOTE

If a junk e-mail folder does not exist, you may receive a message asking if you want to create one. Click on Yes to create the folder, or No to Cancel.

TIP

Choosing to automatically move junk messages to the Deleted Items folder is the same as deleting all junk e-mail automatically.

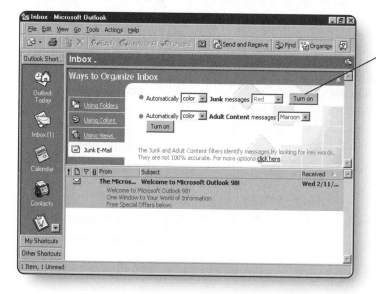

4. **Click** on the **Turn on button**.

When the junk e-mail rule is activated, the Turn on button changes to a Turn off button. To deactivate your rule, click on the Turn off button.

5. **Repeat steps 2** through **4** for adult-content e-mail.

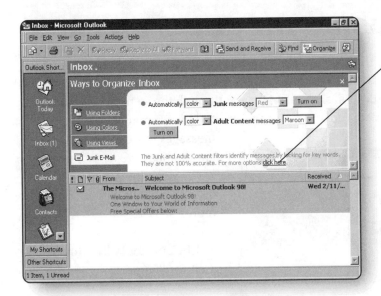

TIP

Outlook uses special rules to determine what is junk or adult-content e-mail. Click on For more options click here for more information about junk and adult-content e-mail.

6. Click on **Organize**. The Ways to Organize Inbox pane will close.

Adding Names to the Junk E-mail List

Even after you have activated junk e-mail rules, certain junk messages may slip into your Inbox. You can quickly add the senders of these messages to your junk senders list.

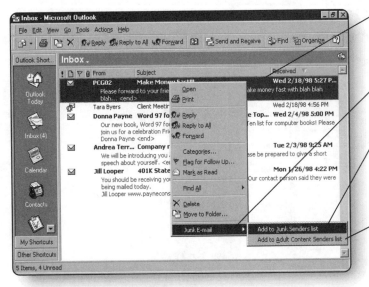

1. Right-click on the offending **message** in the Inbox. A shortcut menu will appear.

2. Click on **Junk E-mail**. The submenu will appear.

3a. Click on **Add to Junk Senders list**.

OR

3b. Click on **Add to Adult Content Senders list**.

USING THE RULES WIZARD

In the previous exercise, you created a *rule* to do something with junk or adult-content e-mail messages. Outlook has a Rules Wizard that walks you through the steps needed to create rules. Rules can be created to automatically move messages to a certain folder, automatically reply to messages, notify you when important messages arrive, and much more.

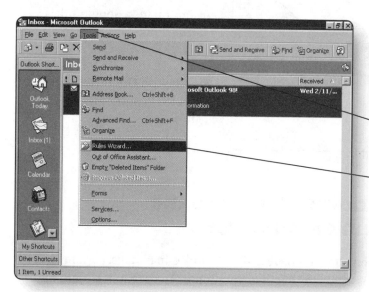

1. Click on **Tools**. The Tools menu will appear.

2. Click on **Rules Wizard**. The Rules Wizard dialog box will open.

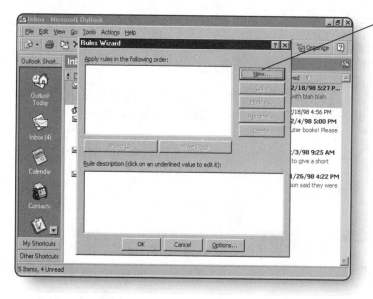

3. Click on the **New button**. The Rules Wizard will appear.

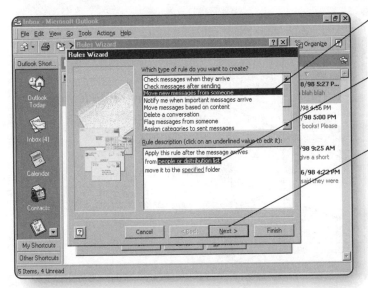

4. **Click** on the **type of rule** you want to create.

5. **Click** on the **underlined options** to edit the rule description.

6. **Click** on **Next**.

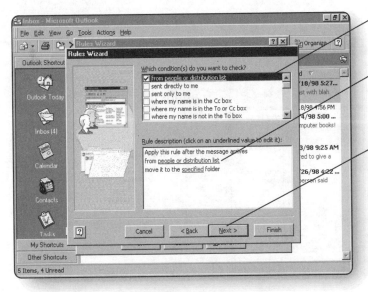

7. **Click** on a **check box** to select a condition.

8. **Click** on the **underlined options** to edit the rules description.

9. **Click** on **Next**.

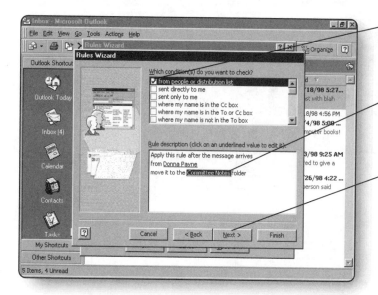

10. Click on a **check box** to select what Outlook should do with the message.

11. Click on the **underlined options** to edit the rules description.

12. Click on **Next**.

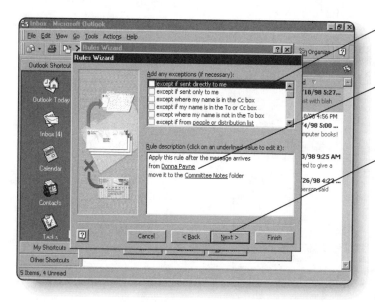

13. Click on a **check box** to select any exceptions.

14. Click on the **underlined options** to edit the rules description.

15. Click on **Next**.

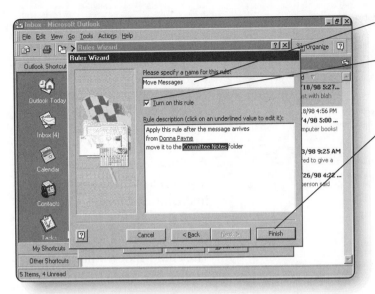

16. Type a **name** for the rule.

17. Click on the **Turn on this rule check box** to turn the rule on or off.

18. Click on **Finish**.

19. Click on **OK**. The Rules Wizard will close.

FINDING MESSAGES

After you have used Outlook for a while, you may have many messages stored in the Inbox or other folders. Outlook has extensive searching capabilities so you can always locate your messages.

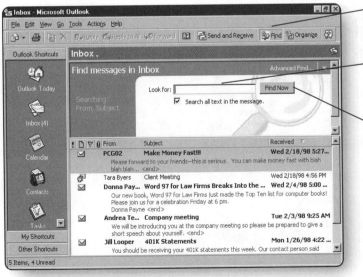

1. Click on the **Find button**. The Find pane will appear.

2. Type **text** in the Look for text box.

3. Click on the **Find Now button**. All messages matching the text you type will be displayed in the Information viewer.

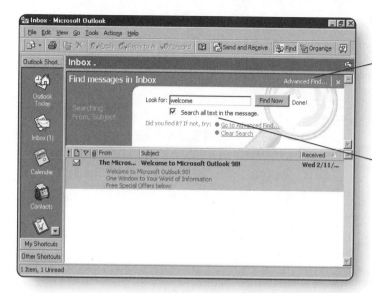

TIP

If you don't find the message, click on the Advanced Find option to specify even more criteria for searching.

4. **Click** on **Clear Search** to display all of the Inbox messages in the Information viewer.

5. **Click** on the **Close button**. The Find window will close.

SORTING MESSAGES

Another way to organize your e-mail is by sorting the messages in your Inbox. Incoming messages can be sorted by several criteria. You can view your messages in the order in which they were sent, by sender, or by several other options.

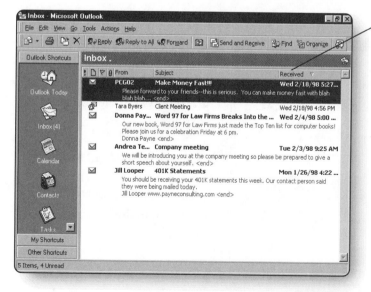

1. **Click** on the **Received column header** to sort all messages based on order received.

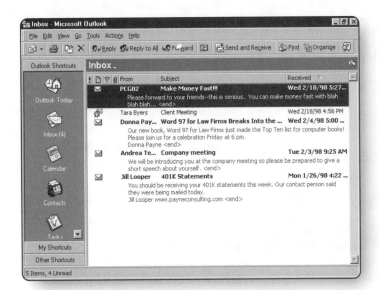

NOTE

The column headers are toggle buttons that let you sort in ascending or descending order. Click once on a column header to sort in ascending order; click again on the column header to sort in descending order. The small gray triangle to the right of the column header indicates ascending or descending order.

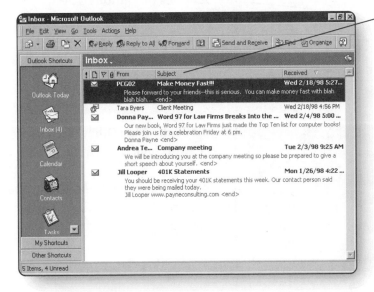

2. Click on the **Subject column header** to sort all messages based on subject.

TIP

You can use many fields to sort; however, not all of them appear in the Information viewer. Click on View, Current View, Customize Current View, and Fields to change which fields are displayed.

ARCHIVING MESSAGES AUTOMATICALLY

Outlook will occasionally poll your mailbox to determine whether it is time to archive. *Archiving* is the process of moving messages from the Inbox to another file. These messages are still available to you after they have been archived. Archiving helps to prevent cluttered or outdated materials from being stored in your everyday mailbox.

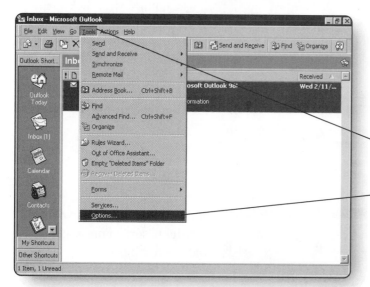

1. Click on **Tools**. The Tools menu will appear.

2. Click on **Options**. The Options dialog box will open.

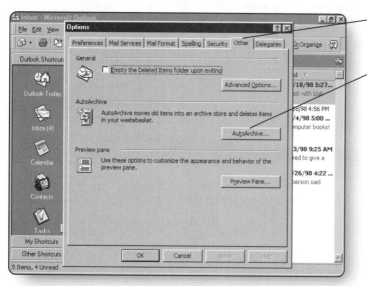

3. Click on the **Other tab**. The tab will come to the front.

4. Click on the **AutoArchive button**. The AutoArchive dialog box will open.

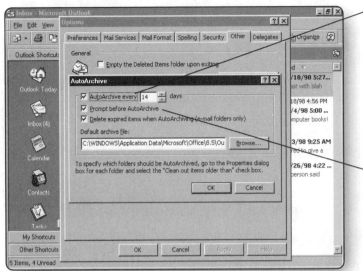

✦ **AutoArchive every 14 days**. Outlook will automatically archive according to the number of days set here. Click on the up or down arrows next to the number of days to increase or decrease the number of days.

✦ **Prompt before AutoArchive**. Before archiving, Outlook will display a message with an option to cancel that particular day's scheduled archiving.

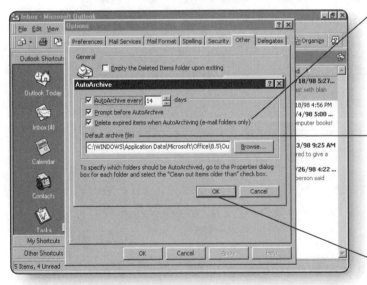

✦ **Deleted expired items when AutoArchiving (e-mail folders only)**. Outlook will delete any expired e-mail messages instead of archiving the messages.

✦ **Default archive file**. The storage location for archived messages.

5. Click on the **options** you want to use.

6. Click on **OK**. Your AutoArchive settings will update if you've made changes.

PART II REVIEW QUESTIONS

1. How do you insert an automatic signature into your e-mail message? *See "Adding an Automatic Signature" in Chapter 5*

2. How do you attach a file to an e-mail message? *See "Attaching a File" in Chapter 5*

3. How do you send an e-mail message? *See "Sending a Mail Message" in Chapter 6*

4. How do you recall a message from the recipient's Inbox? *See "Recalling a Message" in Chapter 6*

5. How do you deliver a message at a specific time? *See "Delivering a Message at a Specific Time" in Chapter 7*

6. Name two methods for previewing the content of an e-mail message without opening the message. *See "Using AutoPreview" in Chapter 8*

7. Name three choices for responding to an e-mail message? *See "Responding to E-mail Messages" in Chapter 8*

8. How do you add an address to the Address Book from a message you have received? *See "Using Addresses from Messages You Have Received" in Chapter 9*

9. How do you add names to the junk e-mail list? *See "Adding Names to the Junk E-mail List" in Chapter 10*

10. How do you find a message? *See "Finding Messages" in Chapter 10*

PART III
Scheduling with the Calendar

11 Viewing Your Calendar

When scheduling appointments, it is sometimes necessary to see what is going on around the same time period but in a different calendar format. Outlook keeps your calendar of appointments and provides you with the flexibility to view your calendar in many different ways. In this chapter, you'll learn how to:

+ Show different calendar views

+ Use Organize to select different calendar views

+ Create your own views

+ Use the Date Navigator

+ Move to dates in the past or future

SHOWING DIFFERENT CALENDAR VIEWS

There are three primary calendar views in Outlook: daily, weekly, and monthly. When you want to choose any of these views, you click on the corresponding toolbar button or menu command. Use views to control what appears on your screen.

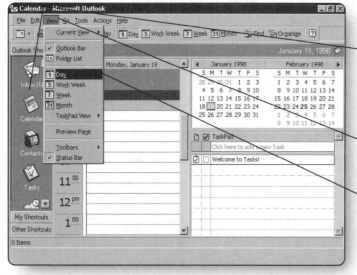

1. Click on the **Calendar icon** on the Outlook bar. The Outlook calendar view will show in the Information viewer.

2. Click on **View**. The View menu will appear.

3. Click on **Day, Work Week, Week,** or **Month**. Your calendar will change accordingly.

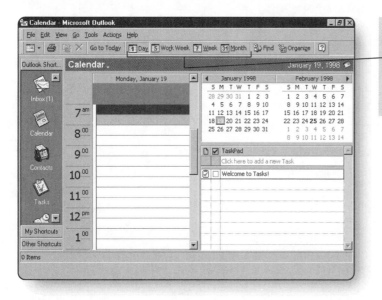

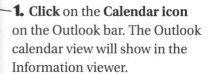

TIP

The Standard toolbar contains buttons to quickly select these views.

USING ORGANIZE TO CHANGE VIEWS

Outlook has a feature called Organize that lets you arrange your calendar. There are two ways to organize the calendar: by categories or by views. *Categories* are words or phrases (such as Business or Personal) used to keep track of items in Outlook.

1. **Click** on **Organize**. The Ways to Organize Calendar pane will appear.

2. **Click** on **Using Categories**. The Organize pane will change, allowing you to organize your appointments by category.

3. **Click** on **any item(s)** in the calendar. The item(s) will appear selected.

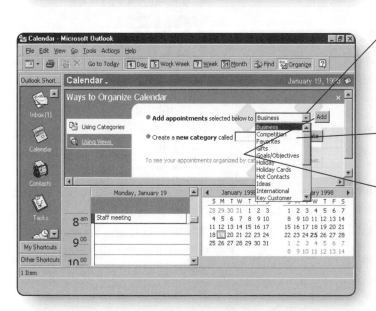

4. **Click** on the **down arrow (▼)** next to Add appointments selected below to. A drop-down list will appear.

5. **Click** on any **category** in the drop-down list.

6. **Click** on the **Add button**. A message saying "Done!" will appear to the right of the Add button and the appointment(s) you've selected will be added to the category you chose.

Adding Categories

Outlook comes with numerous categories, but you can always add more.

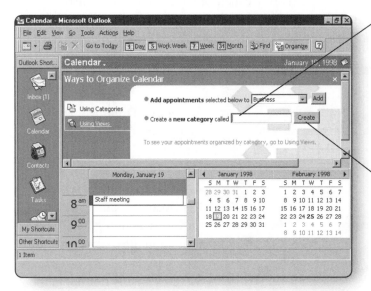

1. **Click** in the **text box** next to Create a new category called. The cursor will appear in the text box.

2. **Type** the **name** of the new category. The name will appear in the text box.

3. **Click** on **Create**. A message saying "Done!" will appear to the right of the Create button and your category will be created. Once this is done, you can add items in the calendar to the new category.

CHANGING YOUR CALENDAR VIEW

By changing your calendar view, you can control the look of the calendar. Some views apply filters, which will display only certain items in the calendar, such as active appointments.

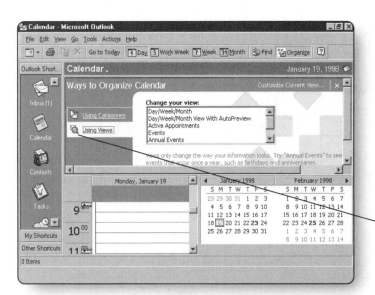

1. **Click** on **Using Views**. Your Organize pane will change, allowing you to organize your appointments visually.

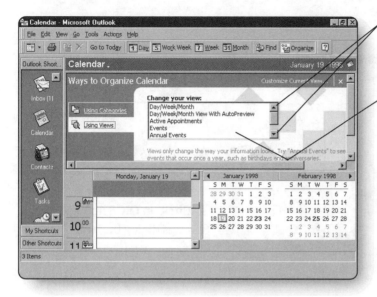

2. Click on the **up** or **down arrow** (◆) to scroll through the list of views.

3. Click on any **view**. The view will change accordingly.

4. Click on **Organize**. The Organize pane will close.

Creating Your Own Views

If the Outlook views do not provide the options you want, you can create your own views.

1. Click on **View**. The View menu will appear.

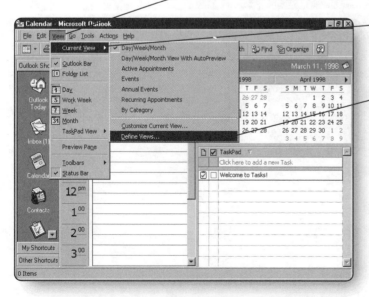

2. Click on **Current View**. The Current View submenu will appear.

3. Click on **Define Views**. The Define Views for Calendar dialog box will open.

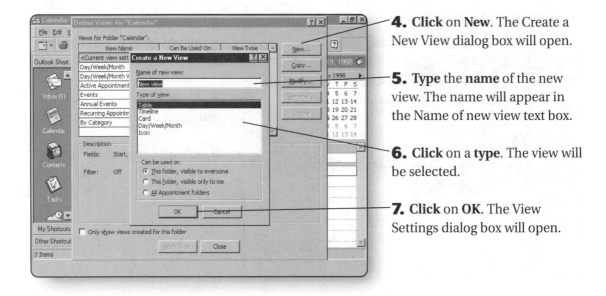

4. **Click** on **New**. The Create a New View dialog box will open.

5. **Type** the **name** of the new view. The name will appear in the Name of new view text box.

6. **Click** on a **type**. The view will be selected.

7. **Click** on **OK**. The View Settings dialog box will open.

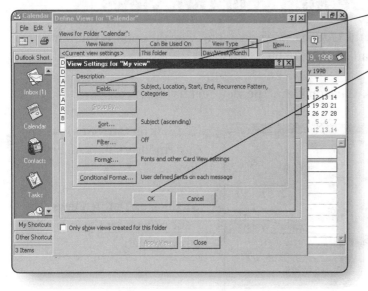

8. **Click** on the **buttons** to choose the view settings.

9. **Click** on **OK**. The View Settings dialog box will close.

USING THE DATE NAVIGATOR

The Date Navigator appears in the right corner of the calendar. A red box appears around today's date, and any day with items scheduled appear in bold. You can use the Date Navigator to jump to any date in the calendar to schedule an appointment or an event.

Viewing Different Months

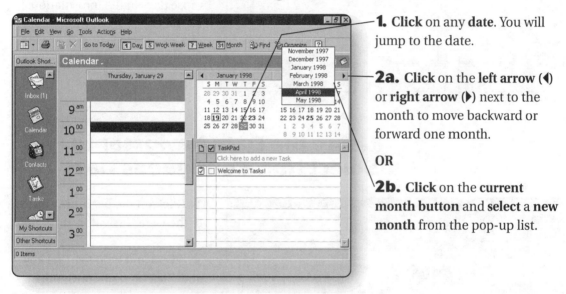

1. **Click** on any **date**. You will jump to the date.

2a. **Click** on the **left arrow (◀)** or **right arrow (▶)** next to the month to move backward or forward one month.

OR

2b. **Click** on the **current month button** and **select** a **new month** from the pop-up list.

Using the Date Navigator to Select a Series of Days

The Date Navigator can also be used to change the days displayed on the calendar. If one of the pre-defined day, week, or month views doesn't fit your needs, you can use the Date Navigator to customize the days displayed in the calendar.

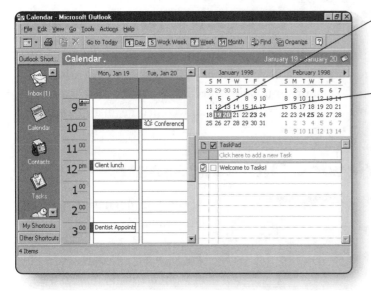

1. **Click** on the **beginning date** in the Date Navigator. The date will be selected.

2. **Press** the **Shift key** and **click** on the **ending date** in the Date Navigator. All dates from the initial date to the ending date will be selected, and you will see those days in the Information viewer.

Using the Date Navigator to Select Non-Contiguous Days

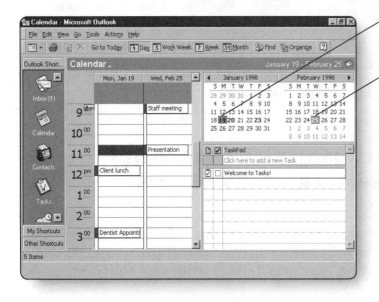

1. **Click** on the **beginning date** in the Date Navigator.

2. **Press and hold** the **Ctrl key** and **click** on **non-contiguous days** in the calendar. Only those days will be selected.

GOING TO A SPECIFIC DATE

If the date you want doesn't appear in the Date Navigator, you can use the Go to Date feature to display a particular date. Go to Date can also be used when you do not know the exact calendar date, but you know that it occurs three weeks from today or on a certain holiday.

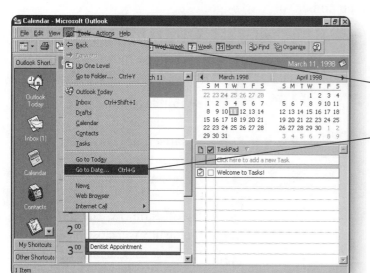

1. **Click** on **Go**. The Go menu will appear.

2. **Click** on **Go to Date**. The Go To Date dialog box will open.

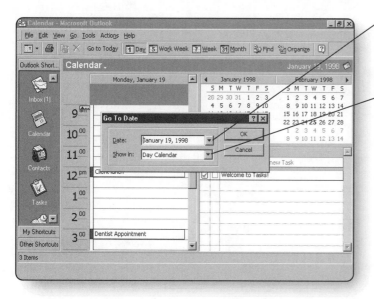

3. **Click** on the **down arrow** (▼) next to Date and **select** a particular **date**.

4. **Click** on the **down arrow** (▼) next to Show in and **select** a **view**.

If you don't know the particular date, there are numerous phrases you can type in the Date list box on the Go To Date dialog box. Here are a few you might find helpful:

✦ **Dates**. You can type "5 weeks from today," "1st week in September," or "3 wks ago."

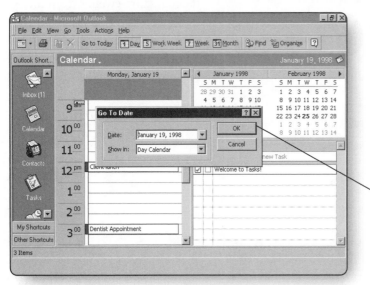

✦ **Description of Dates**. You can type "now," "today," "yesterday," or "last week."

✦ **Holidays**. You can type any holidays that occur at the same time every year, such as President's Day, Boxing Day, or Cinco de Mayo.

5. **Click** on **OK**. The Go To Date dialog box will close and you will return to the Calendar.

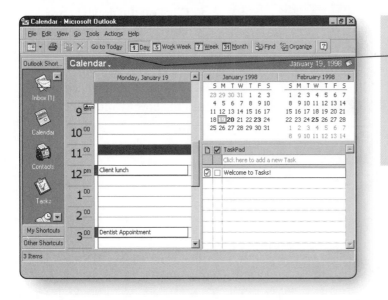

TIP

After using the Date Navigator, you may need to return to today's date. Click on the Go to Today button to return the calendar to the current date.

12 Scheduling Appointments

It's difficult to remember and keep track of all of the appointments and obligations on your calendar. When you use Outlook to manage your appointments, you can keep them all in one location and quickly edit or delete them, should the appointment be changed or canceled. In this chapter, you'll learn how to:

✦ Create an appointment

✦ Set up a reminder

✦ Move an appointment to a different date or time

✦ Schedule a recurring appointment

✦ Delete an appointment

CREATING AN APPOINTMENT

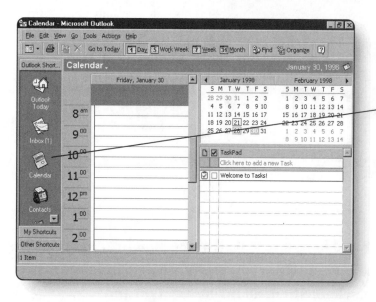

When you want to schedule an appointment in Outlook, you first select the date and then create the appointment.

1. **Click** on the **Calendar icon** on the Outlook bar. The Calendar will show in the Information viewer.

2. **Click** on **File**. The File menu will appear.

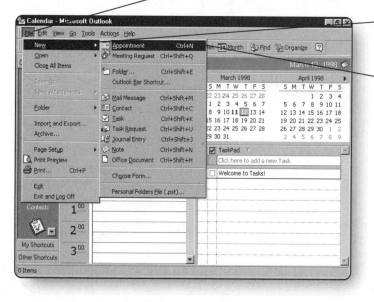

3. **Click** on **New**. The New submenu will appear.

4. **Click** on **Appointment**. The Appointment dialog box will open.

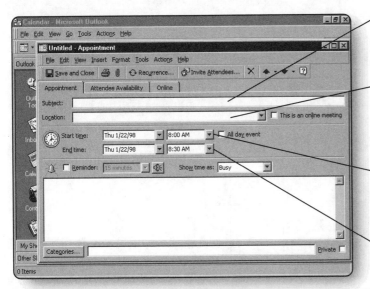

5. Click in the **Subject text box**.

6. Type a **subject**.

7. Click in the **Location text box**.

8. Type a **location** for the appointment.

9. Click on the **down arrows** (▼) next to Start time and **select** a **starting date** and **time**.

10. Click on the **down arrows** (▼) next to End time and **select** an **ending date** and **time**.

Setting a Reminder

A reminder is a great way to guarantee that you won't miss any important appointments. Once a reminder is activated, you can dismiss the reminder or click on the Snooze button and have the reminder pop up again later.

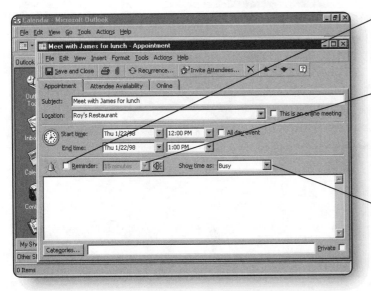

1. Click on the **Reminder check box**. A ✔ will be placed in the box.

2. Click on the **down arrow** (▼) next to Reminder and **select** the **amount of time** the Reminder should appear prior to the appointment.

3. Click on the **down arrow** (▼) next to Show time as and select how the time should appear on the calendar.

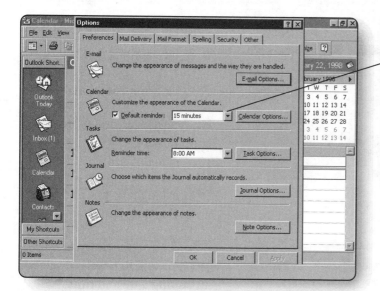

TIP

You can set the default reminder time by choosing Tools, Options, and selecting the Preferences tab. Turn the default reminder off or on and set the default reminder time.

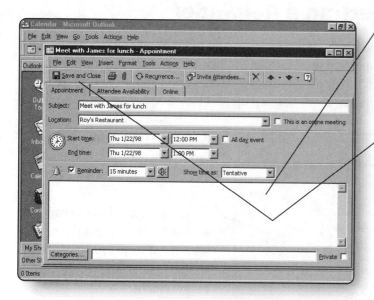

4. **Click** in the **message text box**.

5. **Type** any **notes** regarding the appointment.

6. **Click** on **Save and Close**. The appointment will be saved and closed.

MOVING THE APPOINTMENT TO A DIFFERENT DATE AND TIME

Once you have scheduled an appointment, it's easy to change the time or day of the appointment. Appointments can be dragged to any day on the Date Navigator to reschedule the appointment.

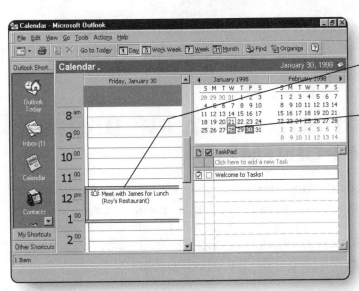
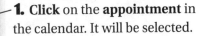

1. **Click** on the **appointment** in the calendar. It will be selected.

2. **Drag** the **appointment** by its border to another day in the Date Navigator. The appointment will be rescheduled.

Changing Appointment Times

You can change the appointment time by dragging the appointment boundaries on the calendar.

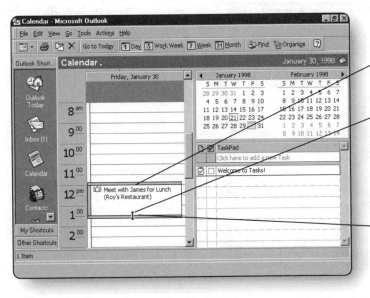

1. **Click** on the **appointment** in the calendar. It will be selected.

2. **Move** the **mouse pointer** over the top or bottom border of the appointment. The mouse pointer will change to a double-headed arrow.

3. **Click** and **drag either border** to increase or decrease the length of the appointment.

TIP

You can change the starting and ending times of the appointment by placing the mouse pointer over the left border of the appointment. The pointer changes to a four-sided arrow, and you can click and drag the appointment to a different time.

NOTE

Another way to change the date, time, or duration of an appointment is to double-click on the appointment. When the appointment window opens, make the necessary changes, and then save and close the appointment.

SCHEDULING A RECURRING APPOINTMENT

A recurring appointment is an appointment that occurs more than once at a regular time. The appointment can occur every day, week, month, or year. Outlook even lets you designate how the appointment occurs (for example, the first Thursday of every month or the 15th of every month).

1. **Right-click** on the **calendar**. A shortcut menu will appear.

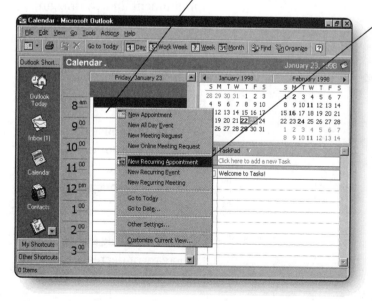

2. **Click** on **New Recurring Appointment**. The Appointment Recurrence dialog box will open.

3. **Click** on the **down arrow** (▼) to the right of Start and **select** a **start time**.

4. **Click** on the **down arrow** (▼) to the right of End and **select** an **ending time**.

5. **Click** on the **down arrow** (▼) to the right of Duration and **select** a **duration**.

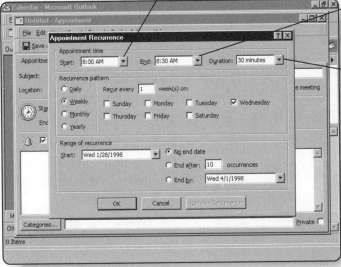

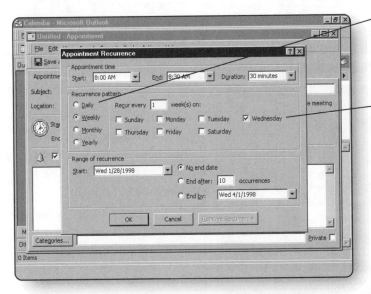

6. **Click** on **one** of the four **Recurrence pattern option buttons**. The option will be selected.

7. **Click** on the **options** to the right of the recurrence pattern to establish the pattern.

NOTE

The window next to the recurrence pattern changes depending on the recurrence pattern selected. Your screen may not look like the figure if you have selected a different recurrence pattern.

8. Click on the **down arrow (▼)** to the right of Start to establish the beginning range of recurrence.

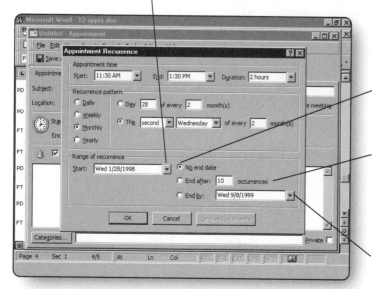

There are several options for ending the appointment. They are:

✦ **No end date**. The appointment will be repeated indefinitely on the calendar.

✦ **End after "x" occurrences**. The appointment will be repeated on the calendar for a specific number of occurrences.

✦ **End by**. The appointment will not appear on the calendar after a certain date.

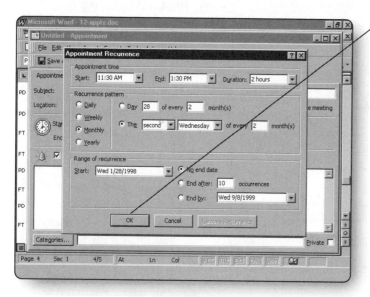

9. Click on **OK**. The Appointment Recurrence dialog box will close.

You can now follow the same steps you followed earlier to fill in the Appointment window. Remember to save and close the appointment when you are finished.

DELETING AN APPOINTMENT

If an appointment is canceled, it's important to delete the appointment from your calendar. If you work with others who may be viewing your calendar to schedule a meeting, it's best to delete appointments as soon as possible if they are not valid.

1. **Right-click** on the **appointment** in the calendar. A shortcut menu will appear.

2. **Click** on **Delete**. The appointment will be deleted.

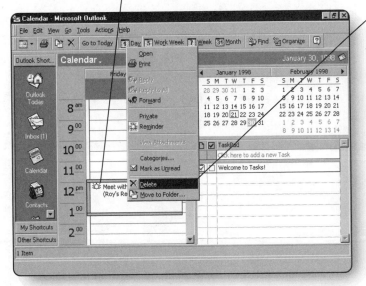

NOTE

If you are deleting a recurring appointment, a message will open asking if you want to delete all occurrences of the appointment or just the one occurrence.

13 Creating Events

You have already learned how to schedule appointments. Events are special types of appointments that last 24 hours or more. Events are a great way to record such calendar items as birthdays, anniversaries, trade shows, or vacations. In this chapter, you'll learn how to:

✦ Create an event

✦ View and modify an event

✦ Schedule a recurring event

✦ Edit a recurring event

✦ Delete a recurring event

CREATING AN EVENT

Events can be split into two categories: an annual event or a standard event. A birthday is a perfect example of an annual event. It occurs on a particular day and it lasts all day. An example of a standard event is a seminar. A seminar can last one or several days. Events can be added to the calendar as easily as appointments.

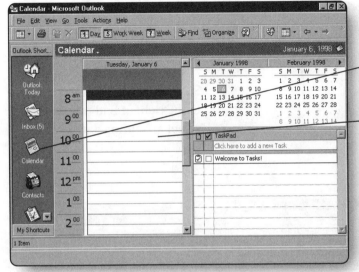

1. Click on the **Calendar icon** on the Outlook bar.

2. Right-click on the **daily appointment area** of the **calendar**. A shortcut menu will appear.

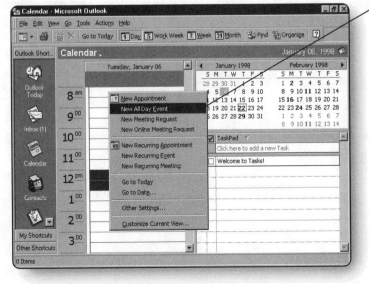

3. Click on **New All Day Event**. The Event window will appear.

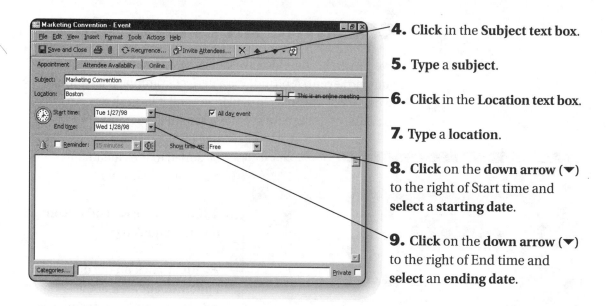

4. Click in the **Subject text box**.

5. Type a **subject**.

6. Click in the **Location text box**.

7. Type a **location**.

8. Click on the **down arrow (▼)** to the right of Start time and **select** a **starting date**.

9. Click on the **down arrow (▼)** to the right of End time and **select** an **ending date**.

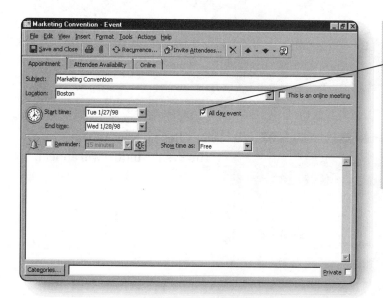

NOTE

The All day event check box is automatically selected for events. If you remove the check mark from All day event, the event will automatically be changed to an appointment.

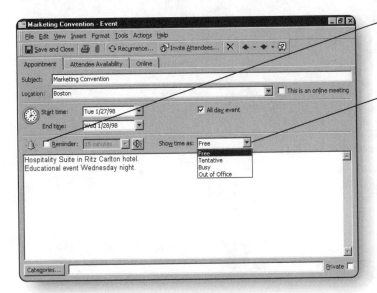

10. Click on the **Reminder check box** to set a reminder. A ✔ will be placed in the box.

11. Click on the **down arrow** (▼) to the right of Show time as and **select** an **option**.

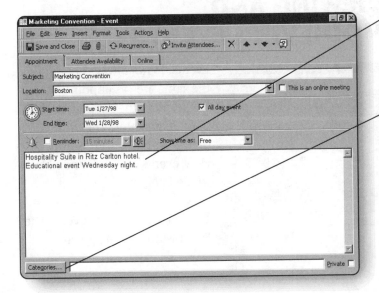

12. Click in the **text area**.

13. Type any **notes** regarding the event.

14. Click on the **Categories button** and **add categories** to the event, if desired.

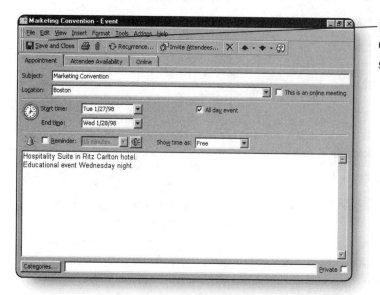

15. **Click** on the **Save and Close button**. The event will be scheduled.

VIEWING AND MODIFYING EVENTS

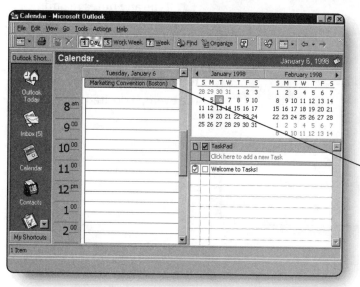

Events do not always appear in the same area as appointments. In Day view, they appear in the banner area, underneath the date. If you are in a monthly view, events are surrounded by a shaded box.

1. **Click twice** on the **event**. The Event window will appear.

2. **Type** any **changes** to modify the event.

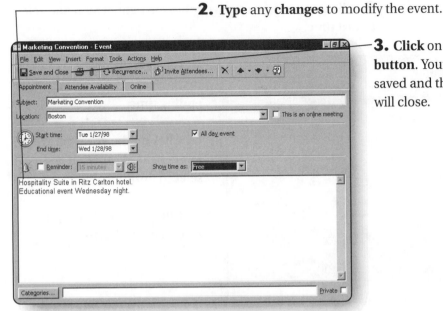

3. **Click** on the **Save and Close button**. Your changes will be saved and the Event window will close.

SCHEDULING A RECURRING EVENT

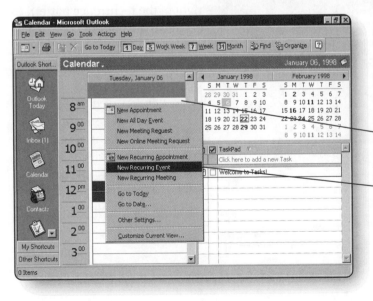

An annual event, such as a birthday, is an example of a recurring event. Events can recur daily, weekly, monthly, or yearly.

1. **Right-click** on the **calendar**. A shortcut menu will appear.

2. **Click** on **New Recurring Event**. The Appointment Recurrence dialog box will open.

3. Click on the **down arrow** (▼) to the right of Start and **select** a **start time**.

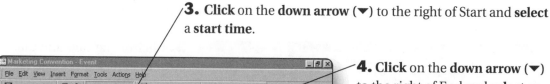

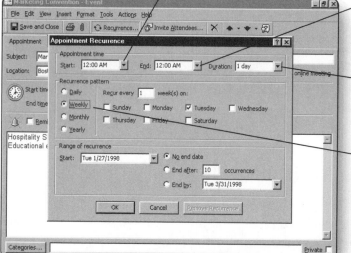

4. Click on the **down arrow** (▼) to the right of End and **select** an **ending time**.

5. Click on the **down arrow** (▼) to the right of Duration and **select** a **duration**.

6. Click on **one** of the four **recurrence patterns**.

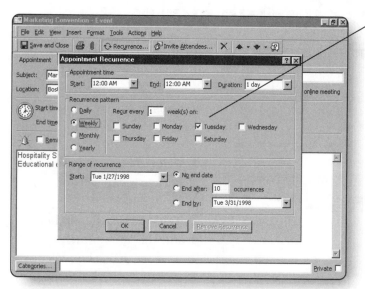

7. Click on the **options** to the right of the recurrence pattern to establish the pattern.

NOTE

The window next to the recurrence pattern changes depending on the recurrence pattern selected. Your screen may not look like the figure if you have selected a different recurrence pattern.

8. Click on the **down arrow** (▼) to the right of Start to establish the beginning range of recurrence.

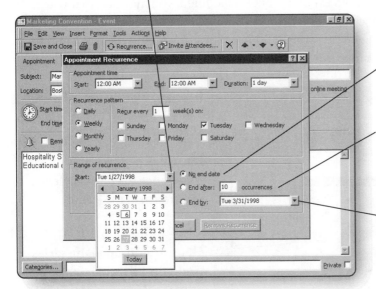

There are several options for ending the event. They are:

✦ **No end date**. The event will be repeated indefinitely on the calendar.

✦ **End after "x" occurrences**. The event will end after a specified number of occurrences.

✦ **End by**. The event will end by a certain date.

9. Click on **OK**. The Appointment Recurrence dialog box will close.

You can follow the same steps you followed earlier to fill in the Event window. Remember to save and close the event when you are finished.

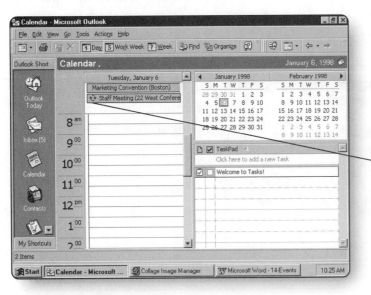

NOTE

Recurring events appear on the calendar with the circular arrow icon.

Editing Recurring Events

After an event has been scheduled, you may find that you need to make changes to a single instance of the event, or to the entire series. Outlook allows you to edit the event and to change the recurrence pattern.

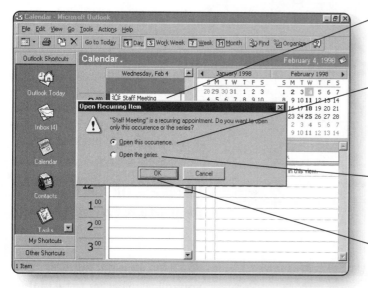

1. **Click twice** on the **event**. The Open Recurring Item dialog box will open.

2a. **Click** on **Open this occurrence** to edit a single occurrence of the event.

OR

2b. **Click** on **Open the series** to edit the series of recurring events.

3. **Click** on **OK**. Either that occurrence of the event or the entire series will open, depending on your choice in step 2.

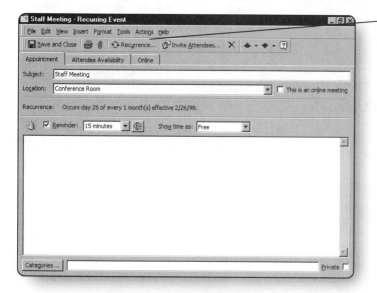

4. **Click** on the **Recurrence button** to change the recurrence pattern of the series.

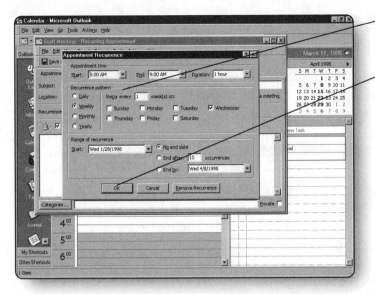

5. **Type** any **changes** to the recurrence pattern.

6. **Click** on **OK**. The Appointment Recurrence dialog box will close.

7. **Click** on the **Save and Close button**. Your changes will be saved and the window will close.

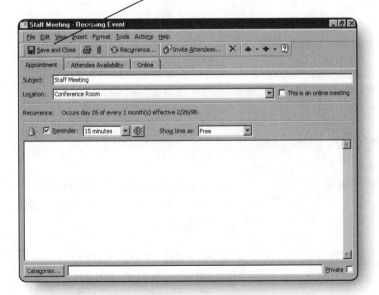

DELETING RECURRING EVENTS

Once an event has been scheduled, you may have reason to delete the event. Do you have to search through the entire calendar, deleting each event? Of course not! Outlook can easily handle the situation for you.

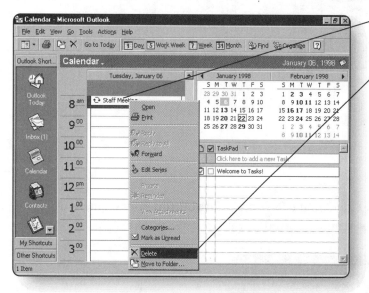

1. Right-click on the **event**. A shortcut menu will appear.

2. Click on **Delete**. The Confirm Delete dialog box will open.

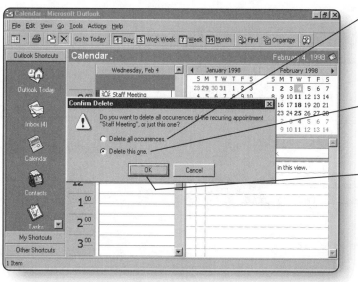

3a. Click on **Delete all occurrences** to delete all instances of the event.

OR

3b. Click on **Delete this one** to delete the one selected instance of the event.

4. Click on **OK**. Either this single event or every recurrence of it will be deleted, depending on the option you chose in step 3. The Confirm Delete dialog box will close.

14 Requesting a Meeting

Have you ever tried to coordinate a meeting with several people? Normally, several calls or e-mails fly back and forth before you can find a time that is convenient for everyone. If you are using Outlook on a network, you can use some powerful tools that are included in the program to take all of the hassle out of scheduling a meeting. In this chapter, you'll learn how to:

✦ Plan a meeting

✦ Create a new meeting request

✦ Schedule a recurring meeting

✦ Respond to a meeting request

✦ Reschedule a meeting

✦ Cancel a meeting

✦ Turn an appointment into a meeting

PLANNING A MEETING

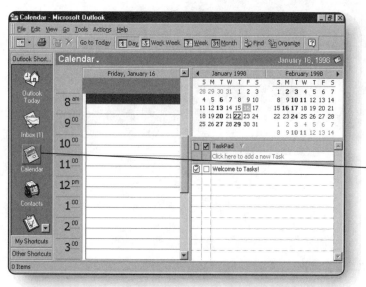

The most difficult part of scheduling a meeting is finding a time when everyone can attend. You can use the Plan a Meeting feature to quickly determine the best time for the meeting.

1. Click on the **Calendar icon** on the Outlook bar.

2. Click on **Actions**. The Actions menu will appear.

3. Click on **Plan a Meeting**. The Plan a Meeting dialog box will open.

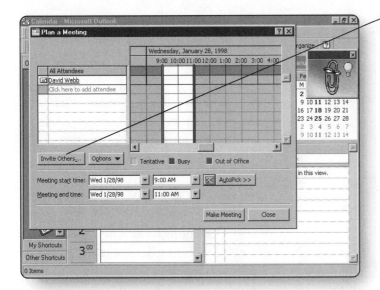

4. Click on the **Invite Others button**. The Select Attendees and Resources dialog box will open.

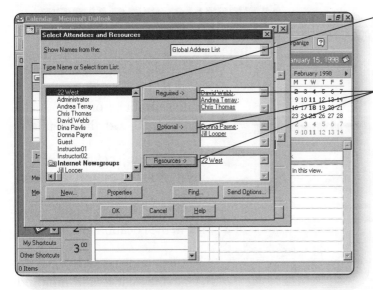

5. Click on a **name** in the address list to select the individual.

6. Click on **Required**, **Optional**, or **Resources**.

NOTE

A resource can be a conference room or a piece of audio visual equipment. Resources appear in the Location box in the Meeting Request. The people who are required or optional will appear in the To line of the meeting request.

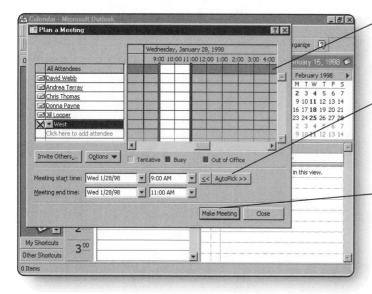

7a. View the **free and busy times** for each attendee.

OR

7b. Click on the **AutoPick button**. Outlook will search for the next available free time for all attendees.

8. Click on **Make Meeting** when you have found a suitable meeting time. A new meeting request will appear.

TIP

If you don't want to use the Plan a Meeting feature, you can send a meeting request by going to the Calendar and clicking on Actions, New Meeting Request.

CREATING A MEETING REQUEST

Now that you have planned your meeting, it's time to invite everyone. A meeting request is a lot like an e-mail message, but it has the added advantage of coordinating with the calendar.

1. Type a **subject** for the meeting in the Subject text box.

2. Type a **location** for the meeting in the Location text box.

3. Click on the **down arrows** (▼) to the right of Start time and **select** a **starting date** and **time**.

4. Click on the **down arrows** (▼) to the right of End time and **select** an **ending date** and **time**.

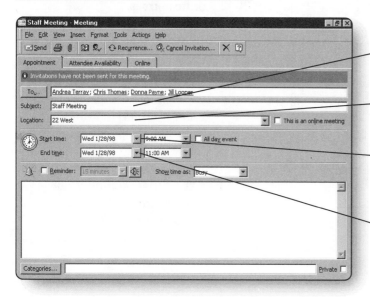

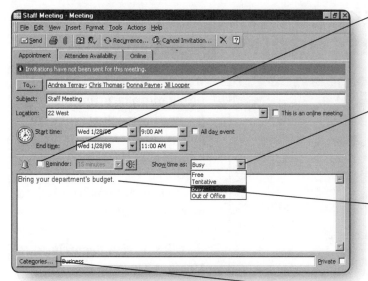

5. Click on the **Reminder check box** to activate a meeting reminder. A ✔ will be placed in the box.

6. Click on the **down arrow (▼)** to the right of Show time as and **select Free, Tentative, Busy,** or **Out of Office**.

7. Type any **notes** in the message text area.

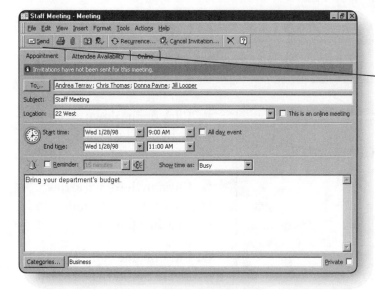

8. Click on the **Send button**. The meeting request will be sent.

SCHEDULING A RECURRING MEETING

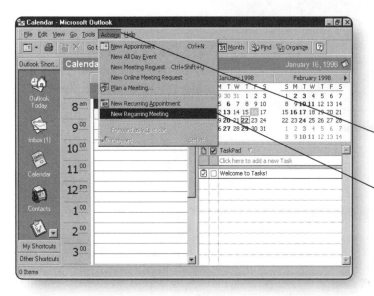

You can take any meeting and turn it into a recurring meeting. A recurring meeting can occur on any series of days, weeks, months, or years.

1. Click on **Actions**. The Actions menu will appear.

2. Click on **New Recurring Meeting**. The Appointment Recurrence dialog box will open.

3. Click on the **down arrow (▼)** to the right of Start and **select** a **start time**.

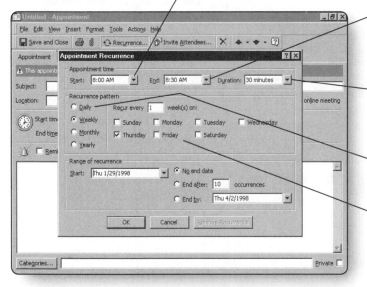

4. Click on the **down arrow (▼)** to the right of End and **select** an **end time**.

5. Click on the **down arrow (▼)** to the right of Duration and **select** a **duration**.

6. Click on **one** of the four **recurrence patterns**.

7. Click on the **options** to the right of the recurrence pattern to establish the pattern.

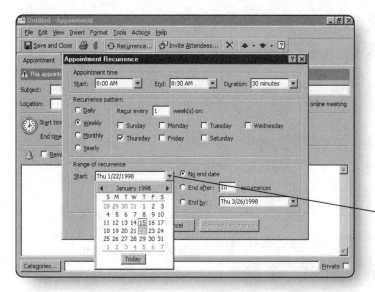

NOTE

The window next to Recurrence pattern changes depending on the recurrence pattern selected. Your screen may not look like the figure if you have selected a different recurrence pattern.

8. Click on the **down arrow (▼)** to the right of Start to establish the beginning range of recurrence.

There are several options for how the recurring meeting will appear on the calendar. They are:

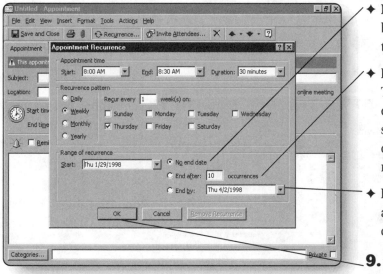

✦ **No end date**. The meeting will be repeated indefinitely on the calendar.

✦ **End after "x" occurrences**. The meeting will not appear on the calendar after a specified number of occurrences. The default number of occurrences is 10.

✦ **End by**. The meeting will not appear on the calendar after a certain date.

9. Click on **OK**. The Appointment Recurrence dialog box will close.

You can follow the same steps you followed previously to fill in the meeting request. Remember to send the meeting request when you are finished.

RESPONDING TO A MEETING REQUEST

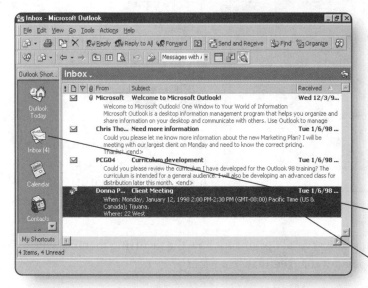

When you receive a meeting request, you have three choices. You can accept, decline, or tentatively accept. If you accept or tentatively accept the meeting request, the meeting will automatically be added to your calendar. If you decline the request, the meeting will not be added to your calendar.

1. Click on the **Inbox icon** on the Outlook bar.

2. **Click twice** on the **meeting request**. The request will appear.

3a. **Click** on **Accept**. A message will open with three options.

OR

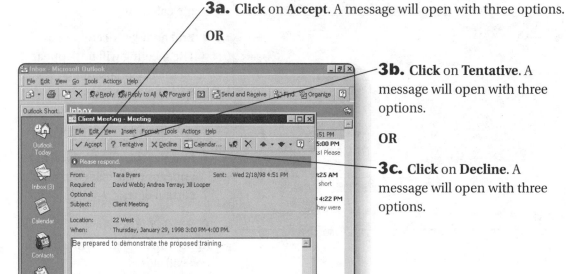

3b. **Click** on **Tentative**. A message will open with three options.

OR

3c. **Click** on **Decline**. A message will open with three options.

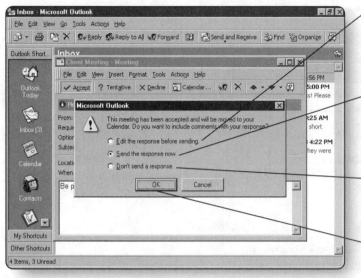

✦ **Edit the response before sending**. Outlook will open a new message window so you can edit your response.

✦ **Send the response now**. The meeting organizer will receive an automatic response that you will not be able to edit.

✦ **Don't send a response**. The meeting organizer will receive no response.

4. **Click** on **OK**. The message window will close, and your choice will be registered. Also, your response will be sent to the sender unless you chose "Don't send a response" from the previous list.

RESCHEDULING A MEETING

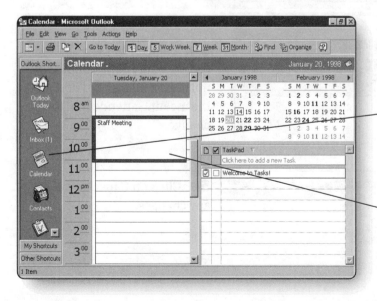

Sometimes a meeting may need to be rescheduled. Outlook gives you a fast and easy way to inform everyone of the change.

1. **Click** on the **Calendar icon** on the Outlook bar. The Calendar will appear in the Information viewer.

2. **Click twice** on the **meeting** in the calendar you want to edit. The Meeting window will appear.

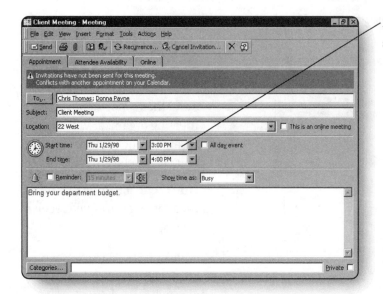

3. **Type** any **changes**, such as start time, end time, or location.

4. **Click** on **Save and Close**. A message box will open.

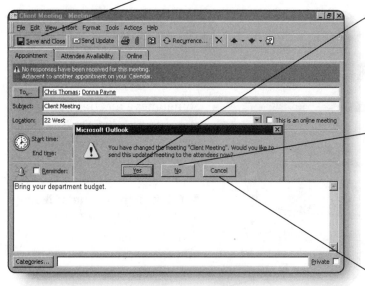

5a. **Click** on **Yes**. The change will be made and Outlook will send a message to update meeting attendees of the change.

OR

5b. **Click** on **No**. The change will be made, but Outlook will not send a message to update the meeting attendees of the change.

OR

5c. **Click** on **Cancel** to cancel any changes.

CANCELING A MEETING

When a meeting has been canceled, it is important to update your calendar so your schedule will be accurate. Canceling the meeting will also update the calendars of the people you invited to the meeting.

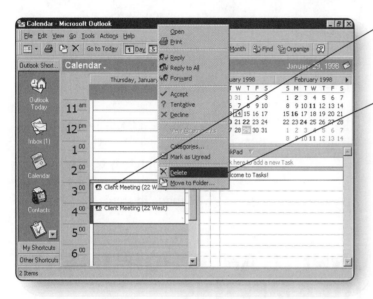

1. **Right-click** on the **meeting** in the calendar. A shortcut menu will appear.

2. **Click** on **Delete**. A confirmation message box will open.

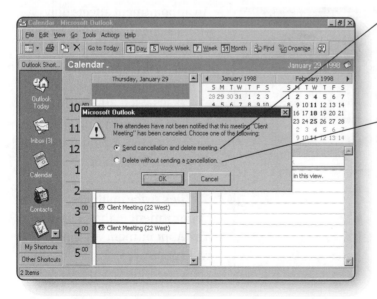

3a. **Click** on **Send cancellation and delete meeting** to notify the attendees.

OR

3b. **Click** on **Delete without sending a cancellation** to cancel the meeting without notifying attendees.

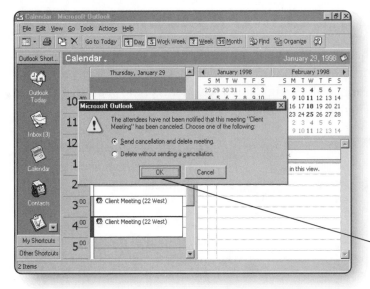

4. Click on **OK**. The meeting will be deleted and a cancellation may or may not be sent, depending on the choice you made in step 3.

TURNING AN APPOINTMENT INTO A MEETING

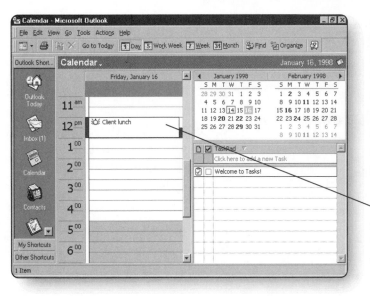

An appointment affects only your calendar, while a meeting involves other people. Occasionally you might have an appointment on your calendar and realize that other people need to be invited. You can easily turn the appointment into a meeting by inviting others.

1. Click twice on the **appointment** in the calendar. The Appointment window will appear.

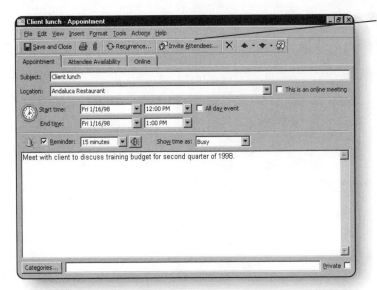

2. **Click** on **Invite Attendees**. A new Meeting window will appear.

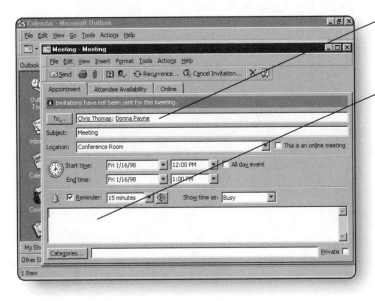

3. **Type** the **name** of the people you want to invite in the To text box.

4. **Type** any **changes** to the appointment, if desired.

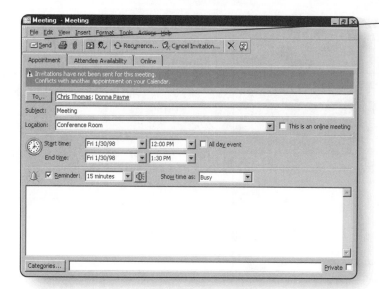

5. Click on **Send**. An invitation to the meeting will be sent to those people you typed in the To text box.

15 Requesting an Online Meeting

If you've ever spent time in an Internet chat room, you have some idea of what an online meeting is like. Many companies are setting up online meetings to have people in different cities attend meetings without incurring the high cost of travel. During an online meeting, you can hold conversations, share documents, look at videos, and even speak to others. In this chapter, you'll learn how to:

✦ Request and attend an online meeting

✦ Make any meeting an online meeting

REQUESTING AN ONLINE MEETING

Filling in an online meeting request is not much different than a regular meeting request. You simply choose a convenient time for everyone and invite others to attend. The main difference is the location—instead of gathering together in a room, people can attend the meeting from their home, office, or any place they have a computer.

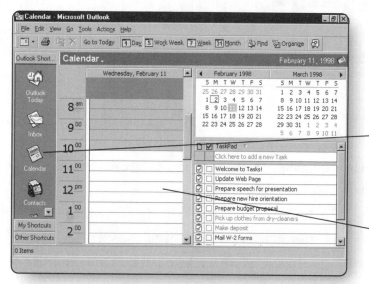

1. Click on the **Calendar icon** on the Outlook bar. The Calendar will appear in your Information viewer.

2. Right-click a **blank area** of the calendar. A shortcut menu will appear.

3. Click on **New Online Meeting Request**. The Meeting window will appear.

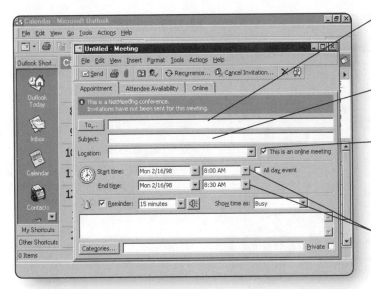

4. Type the **e-mail addresses** of the people you would like to attend.

5. Type the **subject** in the Subject text box.

6. Click on the **check box** next to **This is an online meeting,** if it is not selected. A ✔ will be placed in the box.

7. Click on **Start time** and **End time** to select starting and ending times for the meeting.

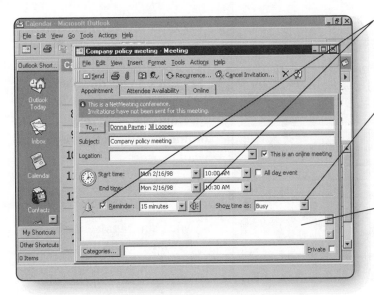

8. Click on **Reminder** and **select** the **amount of time** prior to the meeting for which Outlook should send a reminder.

9. Click on the **down arrow** (▼) next to Show time as and **select** how Outlook should **display the time**.

10. Click in the **text area** and **type** any **notes** regarding the meeting.

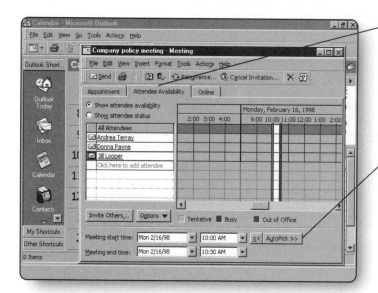

11. Click on the **Attendee Availability tab** and **select** a **convenient time** for all attendees.

TIP

You can click on the AutoPick button to have Outlook search for the next free time for all attendees.

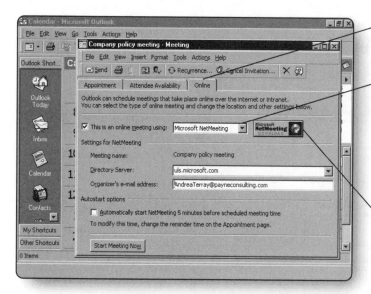

12. Click on the **Online tab**. The tab will come to the front.

13. Click on the **down arrow** (▼) next to This is an online meeting using and **select** the **online meeting software** you want to use.

TIP

Microsoft NetMeeting is free and can be downloaded from the Microsoft Web site. You can click on the Microsoft NetMeeting Download button to obtain the NetMeeting software.

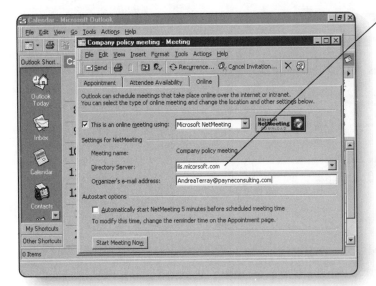

14. **Click** in the **text box** next to Directory Server and **type** a **directory server name**.

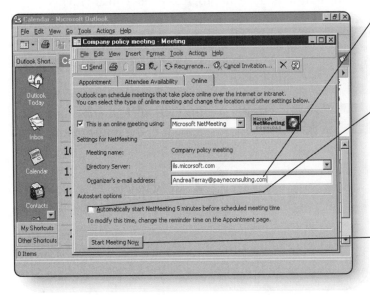

15. **Click** in the **text box** next to Organizer's e-mail address and **type** the **name** of the meeting organizer.

16a. **Click** on the **check box** next to **Automatically start NetMeeting 5 minutes before scheduled meeting time**. A ✔ will be placed in the box.

OR

16b. **Click** on the **Start Meeting Now button**. The meeting will begin.

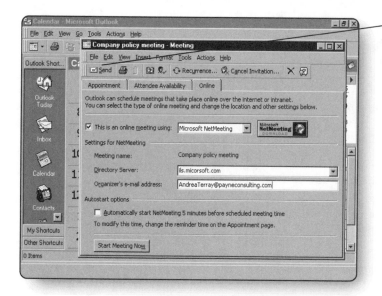

17. **Click** on **Send**. Invitations will be sent to those invitees who are currently online.

ATTENDING AN ONLINE MEETING

When you have been invited to an online meeting, you can respond just as you would for another meeting. An online meeting may already be in progress when you are invited, so it is a good idea to respond to the meeting organizer as quickly as possible.

1. **Click** on the **Inbox icon** on the Outlook bar. The Inbox will appear in the Information viewer.

2. **Click twice** on the **meeting request**. The request will appear.

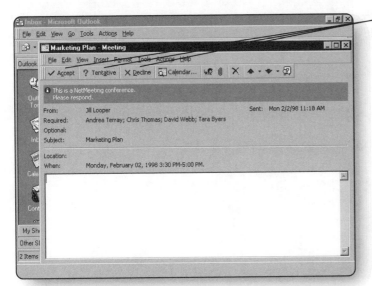

3. **Click** on **Accept**, **Tentative**, or **Decline** to place the meeting in your calendar. Once the meeting is on your calendar, you will be ready to join the online meeting.

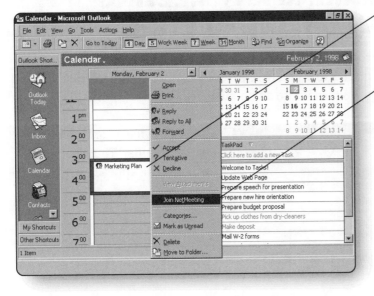

4. **Right-click** on the **meeting** in the calendar. A shortcut will appear.

5. **Click** on **Join NetMeeting**. Microsoft NetMeeting will open.

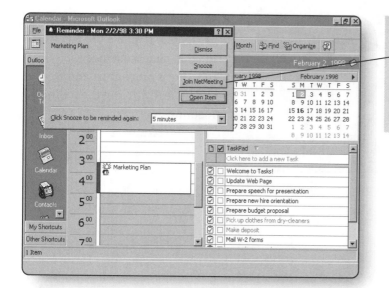

TIP

If you set a reminder, the reminder will automatically include a Join button that you can click.

MAKING ANY MEETING AN ONLINE MEETING

If you have a meeting scheduled and your room reservation is bumped, don't panic! Once a meeting is on the calendar, it's easy to turn it into an online meeting.

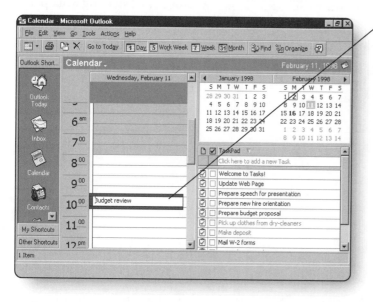

1. Click twice on any **meeting** in the calendar. The Meeting window will appear.

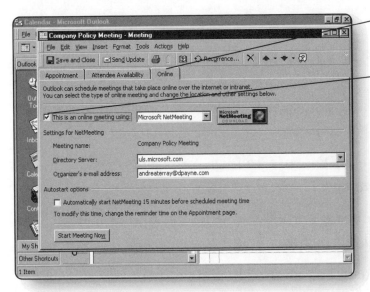

2. **Click** on the **Online tab**. The tab will come to the front.

3. **Click** on the **check box** next to This is an online meeting using: and **enter** the necessary **information**.

4. **Click** on the **Send Update button**. The meeting attendees will be informed of the change.

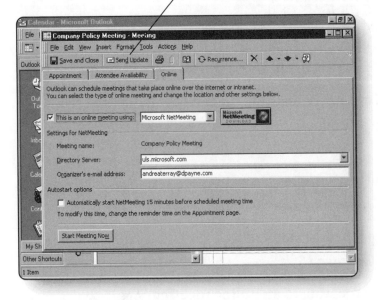

PART III REVIEW QUESTIONS

1. What are the four calendar display options? *See "Showing Different Calendar Views" in Chapter 11*

2. How can you find out the date of a holiday? *See "Going to a Specific Date" in Chapter 11*

3. How do change the default reminder time for all appointments? *See "Setting a Reminder" in Chapter 12*

4. Name two ways to change the date of an appointment. *See "Moving the Appointment to a Different Date and Time" in Chapter 12*

5. Where do events appear in the calendar? *See "Viewing and Modifying Events" in Chapter 13*

6. How would you record a birthday on the calendar? *See "Scheduling a Recurring Event" in Chapter 13*

7. How can you have Outlook determine the next available free time for all meeting attendees? *See "Planning a Meeting" in Chapter 14*

8. Name three possible responses to a meeting request. *See "Responding to a Meeting Request" in Chapter 14*

9. Where does an online meeting take place? *See "Requesting an Online Meeting" in Chapter 15*

10. How do you change a meeting to an online meeting? *See "Making any Meeting an Online Meeting" in Chapter 15*

PART IV

Keeping in Touch with Contacts

16 Creating New Contacts

If you've looked at any business cards recently, you've probably noticed how much information is being included on the card. Everyone seems to have multiple phone numbers, e-mail addresses, street addresses, and even a Web page! Creating contacts is a great way to keep all of this information organized and have it available when you need to get in touch with someone. In this chapter, you'll learn how to:

✦ Create a new contact

✦ View the address map

✦ Create a new contact from the same company

✦ Add a contact from an e-mail message

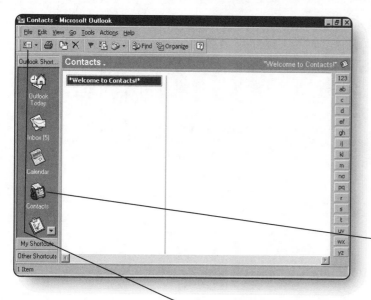

CREATING A NEW CONTACT

It's a good idea to create a new contact record as soon as you meet someone, even if you don't have all the information you need. You can always go back later and update the contact as you receive more details.

1. **Click** on the **Contacts icon** on the Outlook bar.

2. **Click** on the **New Contact button**. A Contact window will appear.

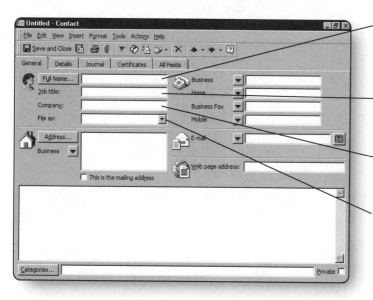

3. **Type** the **name** of the individual in the Full Name text box.

4. **Type** a **job title** in the Job title text box.

5. **Type** a **company name** in the Company text box.

6. **Click** on the **down arrow** (▼) next to File as and **select** a **filing scheme**.

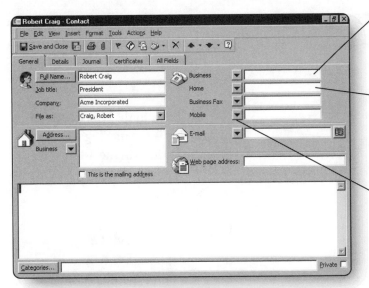

7. Click in the **text box** next to Business and **type** a **business telephone number**.

8a. Click in any of the other **phone number fields** and **type** a **telephone number**.

OR

8b. Click on any of the **down arrows (▼)** next to the numbers and **select** a **different type** of number.

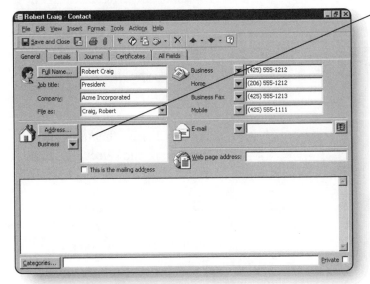

9. Click in the **Address text box** and **type** the **address**.

NOTE

If you do not type the address in a format Outlook can understand, a Check Address dialog box may appear when you exit the Address field. At this point you can fill in more address information and click on OK.

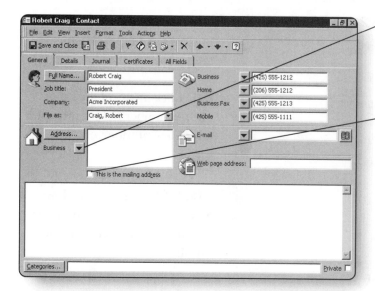

10. Click on the **down arrow** (▼) next to Business and **select** a **different type** of address, if necessary.

11. Click in the **check box** next to This is the mailing address. The address in the Address text box will appear as the mailing address.

NOTE

Mailing addresses are used in other programs, such as Word, when inserting an address from the contact list on an envelope or label.

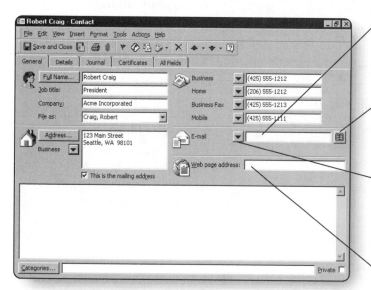

12a. Click in the **E-mail text box** and type an **e-mail address**.

OR

12b. Click on the **Address Book icon** and **select** an **e-mail name** from the list that appears.

13. Click on the **down arrow** (▼) next to E-mail and **add** another **e-mail address**, if necessary.

14. Click in the **Web page address text box** and **type** a **Web page address**.

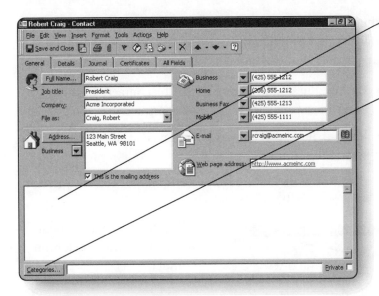

15. **Click** in the **text box** and **type** any **comments or notes** about the contact.

16. **Click** on **Categories**. The Categories dialog box will open.

17. **Click** in the **check box** next to any category. The category will be added to the contact.

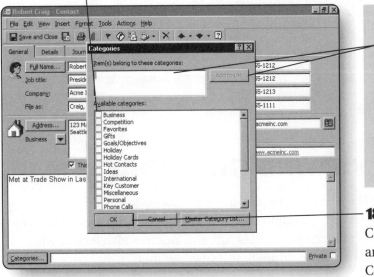

TIP

You can add multiple categories to a contact, or add your own categories. To add a new category, type a category in the Item(s) belong to these categories text box and click on the Add to List button.

18. **Click** on **OK**. The Categories dialog box will close and you will return to the Contact window.

There are many more fields of information that can be added to the contact. Similar fields are organized together on the tabs of the Contact window.

✦ **Details**. Enter information about the contact's birthday, anniversary, spouse's name, or department.

✦ **Journal**. Record details about letters, e-mails, or phone calls sent to the contact.

✦ **Certificates**. If you have added additional security, you can load security IDs in this tab.

✦ **All Fields**. Enter additional fields of information for the contact.

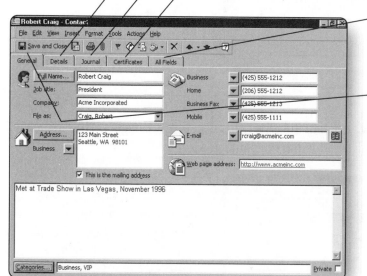

19. **Click** on **Save and Close**. The contact will appear in the contact list.

VIEWING THE ADDRESS MAP

Have you ever needed quick directions to an address? Or perhaps you know where an address is, but you need to locate nearby streets or cities. The new Address Map feature will allow you to do all these things and more.

1. **Click twice** on the **contact**. The contact will appear.

2. **Click** on the **down arrow** (▼) beneath the Address button to **select Business, Home,** or **Other**.

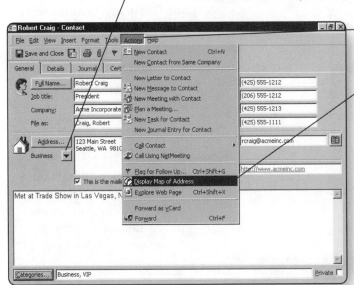

3. **Click** on **Actions**. The Actions menu will appear.

4. **Click** on **Display Map of Address**. Outlook will point your Internet browser to the page on the Outlook Web site that contains a detailed street map of the contact's address.

NOTE

You must have Internet access to connect to the map.

CREATING A NEW CONTACT FROM THE SAME COMPANY

Often, there will be several contacts that have similar information. People who work for the same company often have the same business telephone numbers and addresses. Instead of typing repetitive information, let Outlook do the work for you!

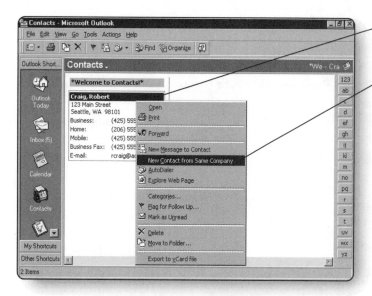

1. Right-click on any **contact**. A shortcut menu will appear.

2. Click on **New Contact from Same Company**. Outlook will open a new contact and fill in the address, business phone, and company name information from the original contact you selected.

> ### NOTE
>
> Outlook will not copy non-business information, such as home address or home phone numbers, when you create a new contact using this method.

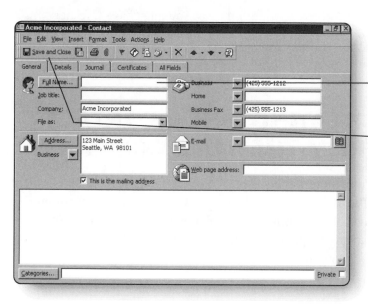

3. Type any **new contact information**.

4. Click on **Save and Close**. The contact will be saved and the window will close.

ADDING A NEW CONTACT FROM AN E-MAIL MESSAGE

What if you receive an e-mail message from someone and decide to add them to the contact list? You don't have to retype the e-mail address—Outlook can take the information and create a new contact for you.

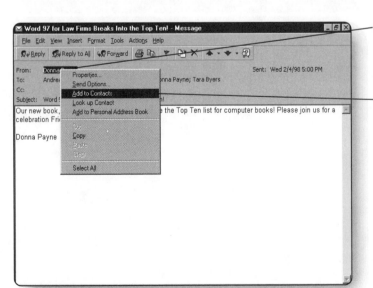

1. **Click** on the **Inbox icon** on the Outlook bar. Your Inbox will appear in the Information viewer.

2. **Click twice** on a **message**. The message will appear.

3. **Right-click** on the **e-mail address** in the From line. A shortcut menu will appear.

4. **Click** on **Add to Contacts**. The Contact window will appear.

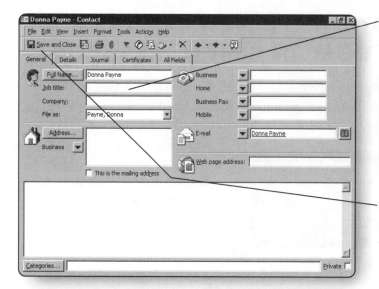

5. **Type** the necessary **information** for the contact.

NOTE

The e-mail address will automatically be added to the contact record.

6. **Click** on **Save and Close**. The contact will be saved and the window will close.

17 Working with Contacts

When you initially fill in a contact record, you may wonder if you will ever use all of the information. Outlook makes it easy to quickly draft a letter, send e-mail, or explore a Web page using the information from the contact record. In this chapter, you'll learn how to:

✦ Edit a contact

✦ Print contacts

✦ Send an e-mail message to a contact

✦ Write a letter to a contact

✦ Explore a contact's Web page

✦ Dial a contact

EDITING A CONTACT

It's rare to have all of the data you need when you initially create a contact. As you receive more details, you can add, edit, or delete any information in the contact record.

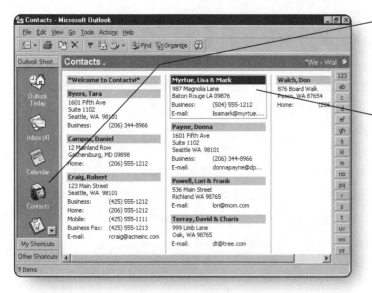

1. **Click** on the **Contacts icon** on the Outlook bar. Your Contacts will appear in the Information viewer.

2. **Click twice** on any **contact**. The contact will appear.

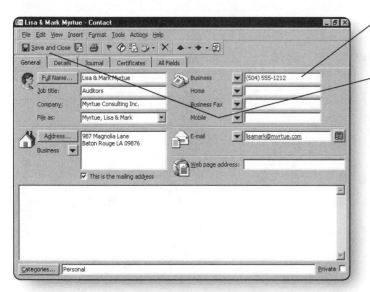

3. **Type** any **changes** to the contact.

4. **Click** on **Save and Close**. The contact will close and the changes you've made will be saved.

PRINTING A CONTACT

If you need a quick list of everyone in contacts, it's easy to generate a printout. Outlook gives you the option of printing one contact, selected contacts, or all the contacts in your contact list.

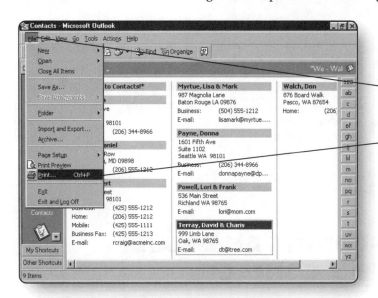

1. **Click** on **File**. The File menu will appear.

2. **Click** on **Print**. The Print dialog box will open.

3. **Scroll through** the **Print style list** and **select** a **print style**.

TIP

A print style can be edited if the style does not meet your needs. Click on Define Styles and select the print style you want to modify. Click on Edit, and make any changes to the font size or style, shading, paper size, and headers or footers.

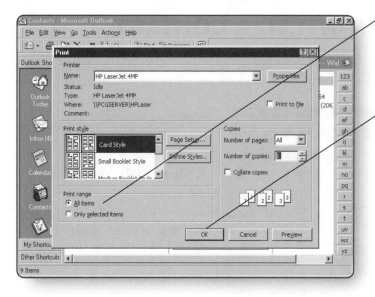

4. Click on the **All items** or **Only selected items option buttons**. The option will be selected.

5. Click on **OK**. Outlook will print all of your contacts, or just the ones you've selected, depending on which option you chose in step 4.

SENDING AN E-MAIL TO A CONTACT

Once you have recorded an e-mail address, it's easy to send an e-mail message to the contact. Outlook allows you to store up to three e-mail addresses for a contact, so you can easily reach someone with multiple addresses.

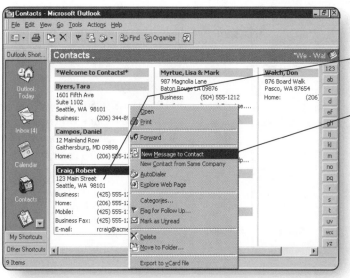

1. **Right-click** on a **contact**. A shortcut menu will appear.

2. Click on **New Message to Contact**. If the contact has an e-mail address, an e-mail message window will open already addressed to that person.

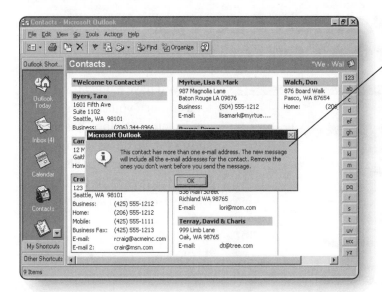

NOTE

If a contact has more than one e-mail address, you will receive a message from Outlook. All e-mail addresses for the contact will be included in the To text box, and you can delete the addresses you don't need.

3. Type the **message**.

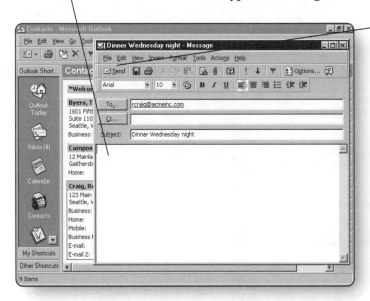

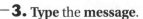

4. Click on **Send**. The message will be sent.

WRITING A LETTER TO A CONTACT

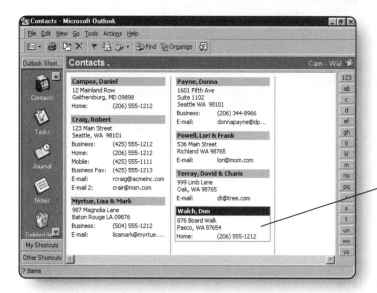

Once you have a postal address for a contact, you can use it to send a letter. Outlook has three addresses: Business, Home, and Other. The address that is marked as the mailing address will be used when sending a letter.

1. **Click** on a **contact**. The contact will be selected.

2. **Click** on **Actions**. The Actions menu will appear.

3. **Click** on **New Letter to Contact**. The Letter Wizard will open.

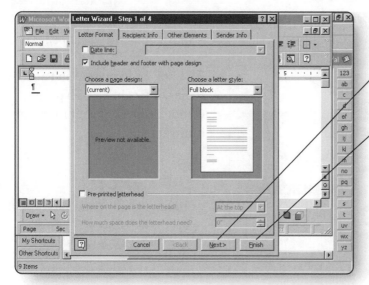

4. **Select** the **options** for the letter.

5. **Click** on **Next** to move through the Letter Wizard.

6. **Click** on **Finish** when you are finished with the Letter Wizard.

NOTE

In Word, you can access the addresses in the Contact list by clicking on the Address Book button in the Envelopes and Labels dialog box.

EXPLORING A CONTACT'S WEB PAGE

Many businesses have Web pages on the World Wide Web that people can access to quickly locate information about their company. Individuals are also creating their own Web pages and loading them on the Internet. Fortunately, Outlook allows you to keep a link to a Web page in the contact record, making it easy to visit a Web page at any time.

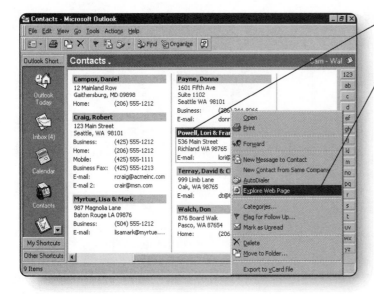

1. Right-click on a **contact**.
A shortcut menu will appear.

2. Click on **Explore Web Page**.
If the contact has a Web page,
Outlook will point your Internet
browser to that page.

NOTE

You must have Internet
access and a Web browser
to explore a contact's Web
page.

18 Organizing Contacts

After you have entered numerous contact records, you may need to organize them. Contacts can be organized by categories, by names, by location, and more. You can also quickly find a contact using Outlook's Find feature. In this chapter, you'll learn how to:

✦ Find a contact

✦ Use folders, categories, and views to organize contacts

FINDING A CONTACT

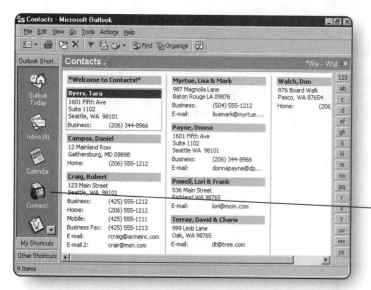

What if you have several thousand contacts and you need to quickly find one? Outlook has a Find feature that leads you straight to what you're looking for. You can even search all the text of the contact if you don't know the exact name or company.

1. Click on the **Contacts icon** on the Outlook bar. Your contacts will appear in the Information viewer.

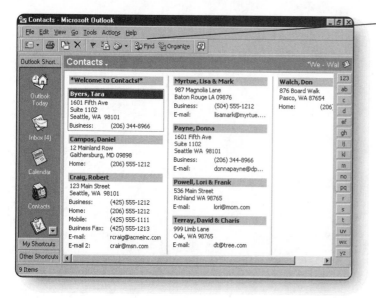

2. Click on **Find**. The Find messages in Contacts pane will appear.

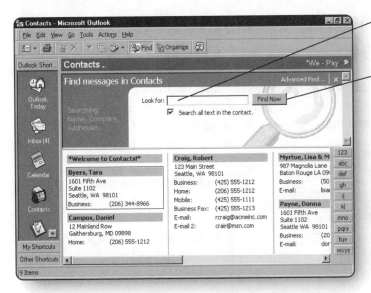

3. **Type search criteria** in the Look for text box.

4. **Click** on **Find Now**.

If Outlook finds a contact record that matches the search criteria, it will be displayed at the bottom of the screen. Click twice on the contact record to display the contact.

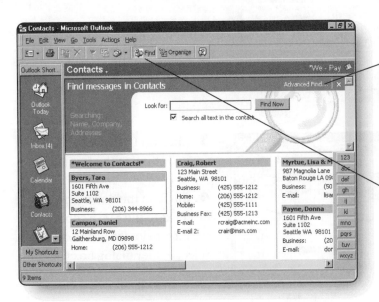

TIP

If Outlook does not find a record matching the search criteria, click on Advanced Find to further refine the search criteria.

5. **Click** on **Find**. The Find messages in Contacts pane will close.

USING FOLDERS TO ORGANIZE CONTACTS

Folders are a great way to organize contacts. For example, you can create a client folder and place the client's contact record in the folder, along with e-mail messages, notes, or tasks related to the client.

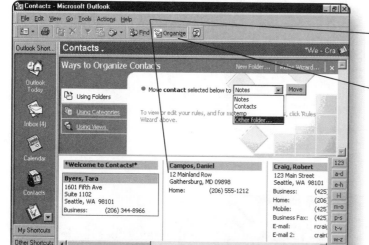

1. **Click** on a **contact**. The contact will be selected.

2. **Click** on the **Organize button**. The Ways to Organize Contacts pane will appear.

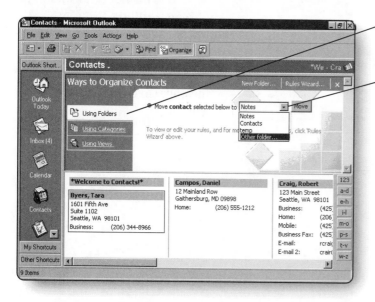

3. **Click** on **Using Folders**. The tab will come to the front.

4. **Click** on the **down arrow** (▼) next to the Move contact selected below to list box. The Select Folder dialog box will open.

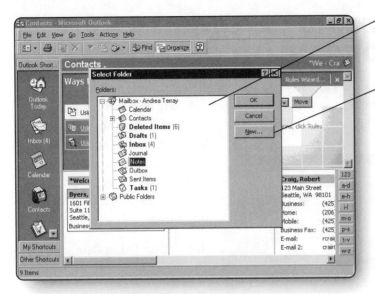

5a. Select an **existing folder**.

OR

5b. Click on the **New button** to create a new folder.

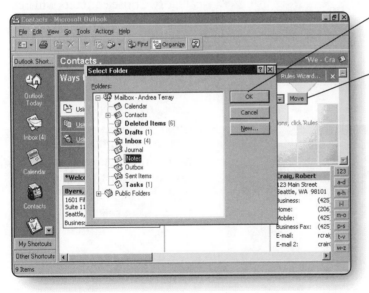

6. Click on **OK**. The Select Folder dialog box will close.

7. Click on **Move**. The contact will be moved to the new folder.

USING CATEGORIES TO ORGANIZE CONTACTS

If you've already entered contact information without categories, you might think it's too late or too much bother to add them now. Not true! Outlook makes it easy to select multiple records and add them to a category. Using this method, you can quickly get your category list up-to-date and organized.

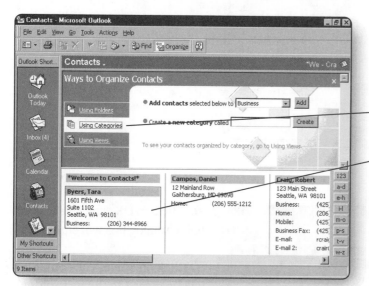

1. **Click** on **Using Categories**. The tab will come to the front.

2. **Click** on the **contact(s)** you want to add to a particular category. Those contacts will be selected.

NOTE

To select a range of contacts, click on the first contact, press the Shift key, and click on the last contact. To select non-contiguous contacts, hold down the Ctrl key and click on each contact that you want to select.

3. **Click** on the **down arrow** (▼) next to the Add contacts selected below to list box and **select** a **category**.

4. **Click** on **Add**. The contact(s) you've selected will be added to the category you've selected.

USING VIEWS TO ORGANIZE CONTACTS

Once you have a large contact list, you may find yourself changing views frequently. Some of the available views are Categories, Company, and Location. You can edit any of the existing views or create your own.

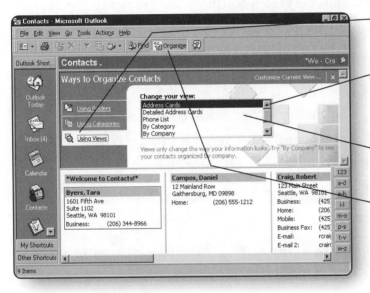

1. **Click** on **Using Views**. The tab will come to the front.

2. **Click** on the **up** or **down scroll arrows** to scroll through the available views.

3. **Click** on any **view**. The view will change.

4. **Click** on **Organize**. The Ways to Organize Contacts pane will close.

PART IV REVIEW QUESTIONS

1. Name the three types of addresses that can be stored in a contact. *See "Creating a New Contact" in Chapter 16*

2. How can you locate an address for a contact? *See "Viewing the Map for a Contact's Address" in Chapter 16*

3. How can you turn an e-mail address into a contact record? *See "Adding a Contact from an E-mail Address" in Chapter 16*

4. Do you have to retype company information when creating a new contact from the same company? *See "Creating a New Contact from the Same Company" in Chapter 16*

5. How do you print a single contact? *See "Printing One or Many Contacts" in Chapter 17*

6. How do you send a letter to a contact? *See "Writing a Letter to a Contact" in Chapter 17*

7. How would you locate a single contact if you know the person's first name, but not their last name? *See "Finding a Contact" in Chapter 17*

8. Why would you want to use folders to organize contacts? *See "Using Folders to Organize Contacts" in Chapter 18*

9. How do you add multiple contacts to a category all at once? *See "Using Categories to Organize Contacts" in Chapter 18*

10. Name three views for contacts. *See "Using Views to Organize Contacts" in Chapter 18*

PART V

Staying on Top of Things with Tasks

19

Using Tasks

With so much work to do, it helps to keep a list of the most important items that need to be completed. Using the task list in Outlook will help you keep all of these items under control, and give you a record of which tasks have been completed. In this chapter, you'll learn how to:

✦ Add a new task

✦ Set a reminder

✦ Update task status

✦ Mark a task complete

✦ Delete a task

ADDING A NEW TASK

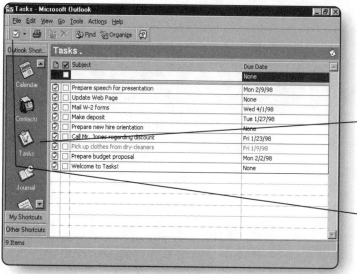

It's easy to add tasks to your task list. You can type directly into the list of tasks, or you can open a Task window and fill in more detail.

1. **Click** on the **Tasks icon** on the Outlook bar. Your tasks will appear in the Information viewer.

2. **Click** on the **New Task button**. A new Task window will appear.

3. **Type** the **subject** of the task in the Subject text box.

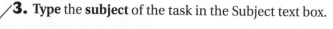

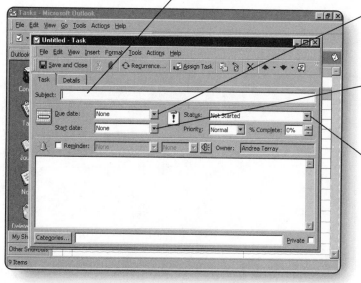

4. **Click** on the **down arrow** (▼) next to Due date and **select** a **due date**, or select None.

5. **Click** on the **down arrow** (▼) next to Start date and **select** a **start date**, or select None.

6. **Click** on the **down arrow** (▼) next to Status and **select** a **status**, or select Not Started.

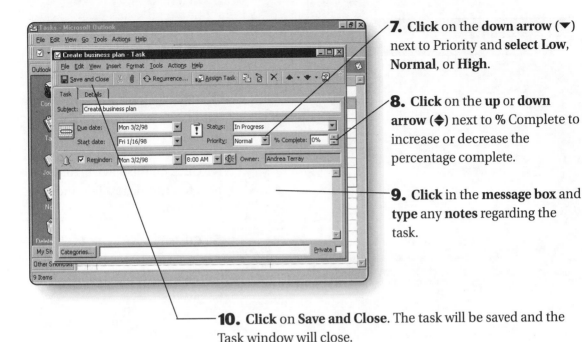

7. **Click** on the **down arrow (▼)** next to Priority and **select Low, Normal**, or **High**.

8. **Click** on the **up** or **down arrow (◆)** next to **%** Complete to increase or decrease the percentage complete.

9. **Click** in the **message box** and **type** any **notes** regarding the task.

10. **Click** on **Save and Close**. The task will be saved and the Task window will close.

SETTING A REMINDER

If a task is important, you may want to set a reminder. A reminder will pop up and let you know that the task is due. You can postpone or dismiss the task when you are reminded.

1. **Double-click** on the **task**. The task will appear.

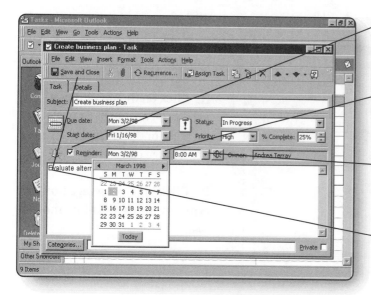

2. **Click** on the **Reminder check box**. A ✔ will be placed in the box.

3. **Click** on the **down arrow (▼)** next to the Reminder text box and **select** a **date**.

4. **Click** on the **down arrow (▼)** next to the time text box and **select** a **time**.

5. **Click** on **Save and Close**. The task window will close and any changes you've made will be saved.

Reminders will only pop up while Outlook is running. There are three options when you have a reminder.

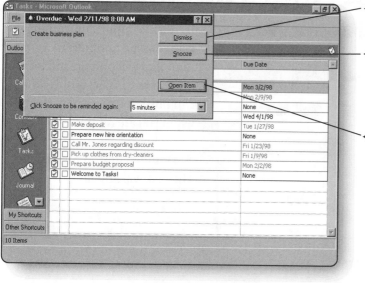

✦ **Dismiss**. Click on Dismiss to close the reminder.

✦ **Snooze**. Click on Snooze to delay the reminder. Select a time in the Click Snooze to be reminded again list box.

✦ **Open Item**. Click on Open Item to open the task.

UPDATING TASKS WITH STATUS INFORMATION

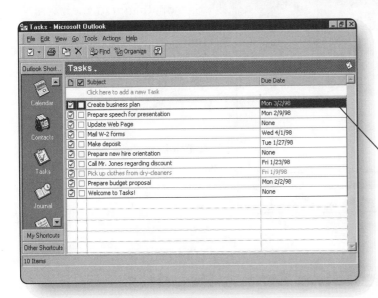

Once a task is on your task list, you can update the task by changing the percentage complete detail. This will help you keep your task list up-to-date.

1. Double-click on the **task**. The task will appear.

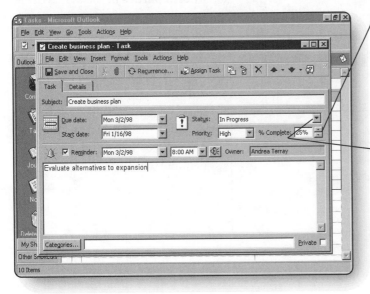

2a. Click on the **up** or **down arrow** (◆) next to % Complete to increase or decrease the percentage complete.

OR

2b. Click on the **down arrow** (▼) next to Status to change the status.

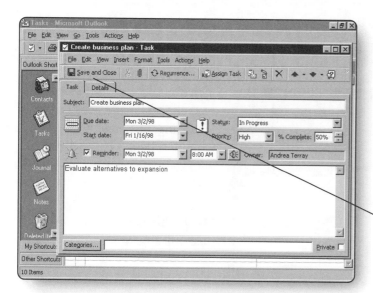

3. Click on **Save and Close** to save and close the task.

Sending Status Reports

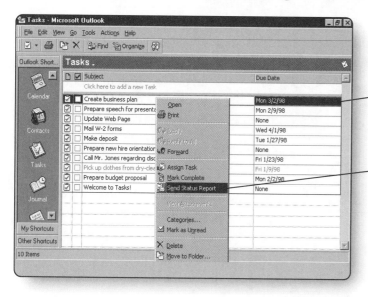

You can send a status report to inform parties of the status of the task.

1. Right-click on the **task** in the task list. A shortcut menu will appear.

2. Click on **Send Status Report**. A new Task Status Report window will appear.

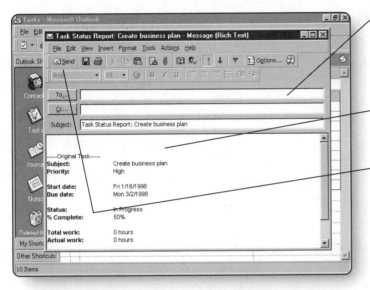

3. **Type** the **e-mail address** of the person to whom you want to send a status report in the To text box.

4. **Type** any **message** in the message text box.

5. **Click** on **Send**. A status report will be sent.

MARKING A TASK AS COMPLETE

When you are finished with a task, you can mark it as complete. A completed task does not disappear completely. It remains on your task list, and you can choose to display the task or not.

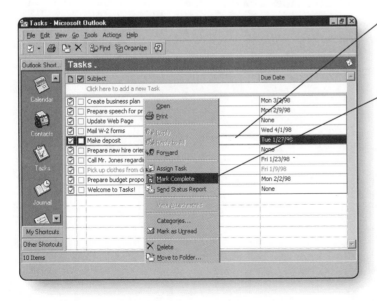

1. **Right-click** on a **task** in the task list. A shortcut menu will appear.

2. **Click** on **Mark Complete**. A check mark will appear next to the task in the task list.

TIP

A quick way to mark a task as complete is to click on the Complete check box on the task list.

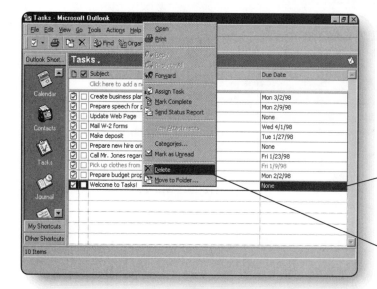

DELETING A TASK

Occasionally a task may need to be deleted. If the task is no longer necessary, you can delete the task to clean up your task list.

1. Right-click on a **task** in the task list. A shortcut menu will appear.

2. Click on **Delete**. The task will be deleted.

20 Assigning Tasks to Others

If you are lucky, you will not have to handle all of your tasks alone. Outlook has a feature called Task Request that lets you assign tasks to other people. They can accept, reject, or assign the task to someone else. In this chapter, you'll learn how to:

✦ Create a task request

✦ Respond to a task

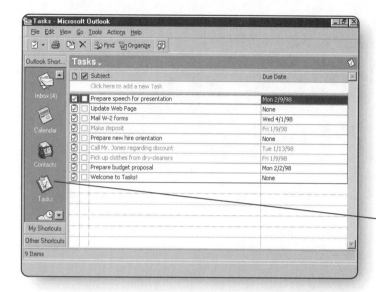

CREATING A TASK REQUEST

A Task Request is a task that you create and then assign to someone else. You can receive status reports so that you know the status of the task and when it has been marked complete.

1. **Click** on the **Tasks icon** on the Outlook bar. Your tasks will appear in the Information viewer.

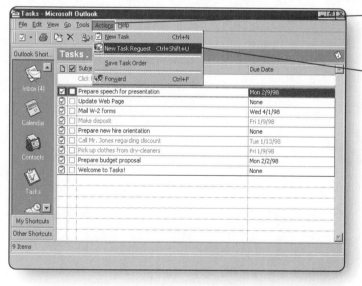

2. **Click** on **Actions**. The Actions menu will appear.

3. **Click** on **New Task Request**. A new Task window will appear.

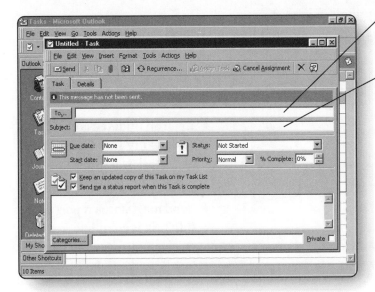

4. **Type** the **recipient's name** in the To text box.

5. **Type** the **subject** in the Subject text box.

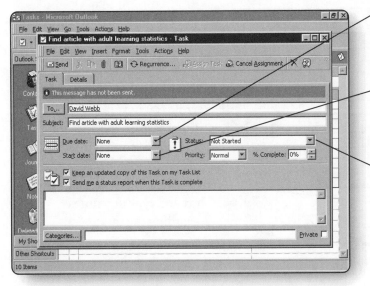

6. **Click** on the **down arrow** (▼) next to Due date and **select** a **due date**, or select None.

7. **Click** on the **down arrow** (▼) next to Start date and **select** a **start date**, or select None.

8. **Click** on the **down arrow** (▼) next to Status and **select** a **status**, or select Not Started.

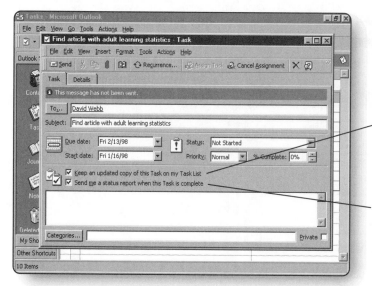

You have some tracking options available when assigning a task, which allow you to receive notification or automatic updates as progress is made:

✦ **Keep an updated copy of this Task on my Task List**. A copy of the task will stay on your task list and get updated.

✦ **Send me a status report when this Task is complete**. You will receive a message when the task is marked complete.

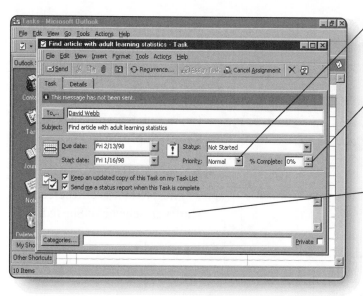

9. Click on the **down arrow (▼)** next to Priority and select **Low**, **Normal**, or **High**.

10. Click on the **up** or **down arrow (⬍)** next to % Complete: to increase or decrease the percentage complete.

11. Click in the **message text box** and **type** any **notes** regarding the task.

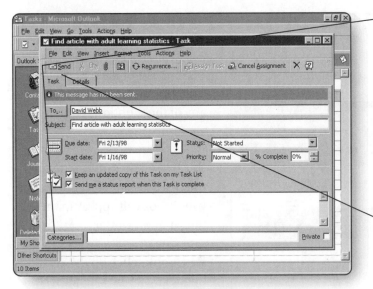

12. **Click** on the **Categories button** and **add** any **categories**, if desired.

NOTE

You may need to maximize the Task Request to see the Categories text box.

13. **Click** on **Send**. The task will be sent to the recipient.

Task Requests will remain on your task list if you have selected the option to keep an updated copy on your task list.

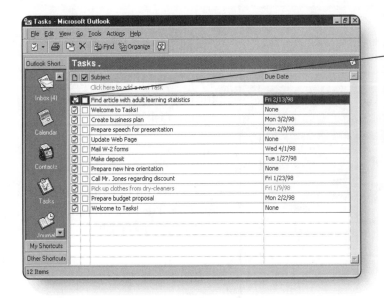

TIP

In the task list, you can distinguish a task from a Task Request by looking at the icon.

RESPONDING TO A TASK

If you receive a Task Request, you have several choices. You can accept the task, reject the task, or assign the task to someone else. Outlook makes any of these options easy to choose.

1. **Click** on the **Inbox icon** on the Outlook bar. The contents of your Inbox will appear in the Information viewer.

2. **Double-click** on the **Task Request**. The Task Request window will appear.

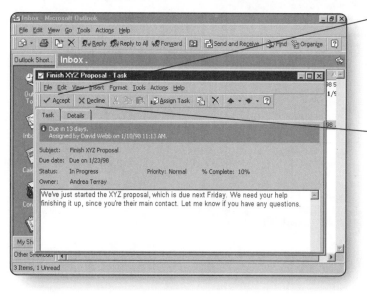

3a. **Click** on **Accept** to accept the task. The task will be added to your task list.

OR

3b. **Click** on **Decline** to decline the task. The task won't be added to your task list.

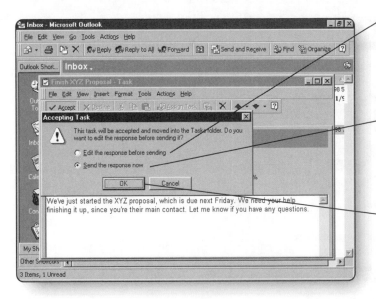

4a. **Click** on the **Edit the response before sending option button** to send a response.

OR

4b. **Click** on the **Send the response now option button** to accept or decline the task without sending a response.

5. **Click** on **OK**. Outlook will either send your response, or allow you to edit it, depending on the option you chose in step 4.

Delegating Tasks

If you are unable to complete the task but can delegate the task to someone else you can reassign the task. When you reassign the task, you give up ownership of the task; however, you can still keep an updated copy of the task on your task list.

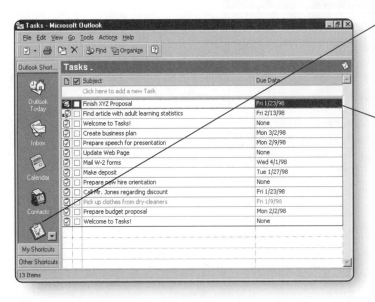

1. **Click** on the **Tasks icon** on the Outlook bar. Your tasks will appear in the Information viewer.

2. **Double-click** on the **Task Request** in the task list. The Task Request window will appear.

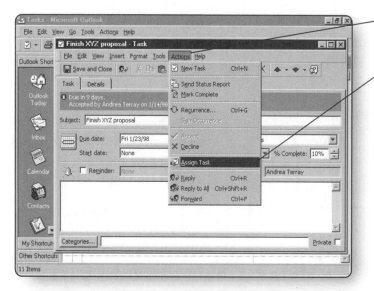

3. Click on **Actions**. The Actions menu will appear.

4. Click on **Assign Task**. A new Task window will open.

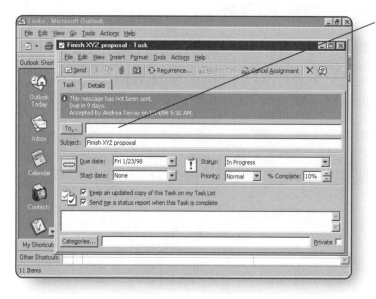

5. Type the **name** of the person to whom you are sending the task in the To text box.

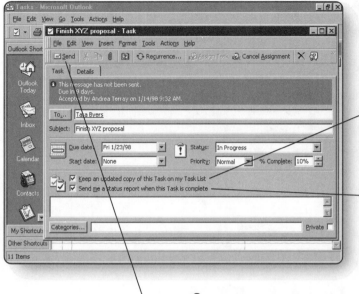

You have some tracking options available when assigning a task, which allows you to receive notification or updates as progress is made:

✦ **Keep an updated copy of this Task on my Task List**. A copy of the task will stay on your task list and get updated.

✦ **Send me a status report when this Task is complete**. You will receive a message when the task is complete.

6. Click on **Send**. The task will be delegated to the person indicated in step 5.

Declining a Task After You Have Accepted It

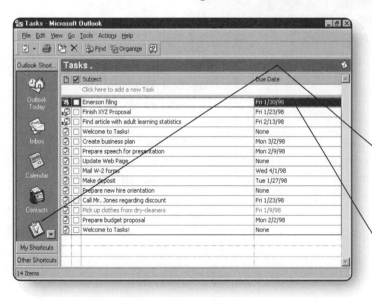

Have you ever bitten off more than you can chew with pending projects? Outlook can help you out of a sticky situation by allowing you to decline a task you had previously accepted.

1. Click on the **Tasks icon** on the Outlook bar. Your tasks will appear in the Information viewer.

2. Double-click on the **task** in the task list. The task will appear.

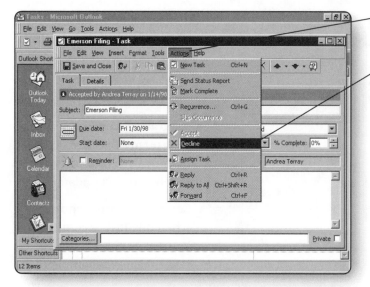

3. Click on **Actions**. The Actions menu will appear.

4. Click on **Decline**. The Declining Task dialog box will open.

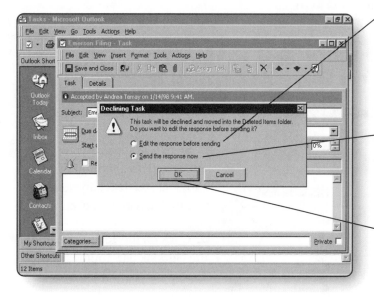

5a. Click on the **Edit the response before sending option button** to decline the task and add a response.

OR

5b. Click on the **Send the response now option button** to decline the task without sending a response.

6. Click on **OK**. Outlook will allow you to edit the task before you send it, or send it immediately, depending on the option you selected in step 5.

21 Organizing Tasks

If you have a long list of tasks, you will need a few tricks so you can see the most important tasks, or the tasks that are due today. Changing views and sorting the task list are fast and easy ways to get tasks under control. In this chapter, you'll learn how to:

✦ Use folders and categories to organize tasks

✦ Change the task list view

✦ Sort and print the task list

USING FOLDERS TO ORGANIZE TASKS

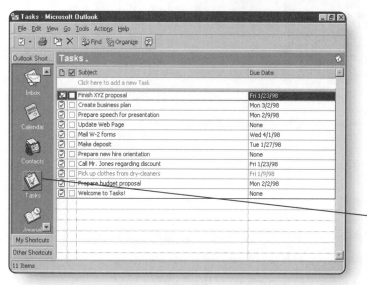

Outlook automatically stores tasks in the Tasks folder. After you have used Outlook for a while, the Tasks folder may grow to contain an enormous amount of tasks. Instead of scrolling through a long list of tasks, you can create subfolders under the Task folder, and view tasks by folder.

1. Click on the **Tasks icon** in the Outlook bar. Your tasks will appear in the Information viewer.

2. Click on **Organize**. The Ways to Organize Tasks pane will open.

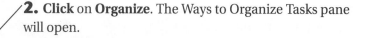

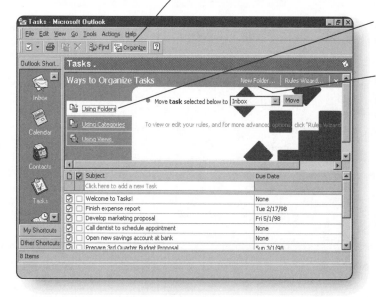

3. Click on **Using Folders**. The tab will come to the front.

4. Click on **New Folder**. The Create New Folder dialog box will open.

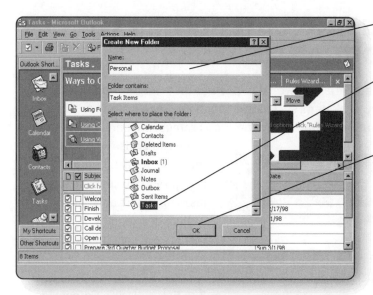

5. **Type** the **name** of the new folder in the Name text box.

6. **Click** on the **Tasks folder**. The new folder will be a subfolder of the Tasks folder.

7. **Click** on **OK**. The new folder will be created.

NOTE

You may receive a message asking if you want a shortcut to the new folder placed on the Outlook bar. If you do, click on Yes; otherwise, click on No

8. **Click** on any **task** in the Task list. The task will be selected.

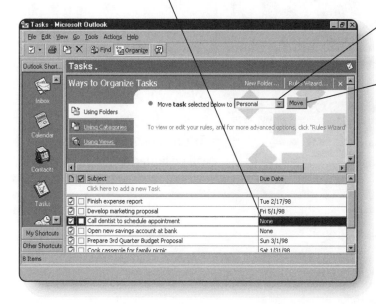

9. **Click** on the **down arrow (▼)** next to Move and **select** a **folder**.

10. **Click** on **Move**. The task will be moved to the folder you selected in step 9.

USING CATEGORIES TO ORGANIZE TASKS

Categories are words or phrases that can be applied to any Outlook item, such as an e-mail message, a note, or a task. Outlook comes with numerous categories, and you can add more categories to customize the category list. Using categories will keep all of the tasks for a particular client or project tied together, and make sorting and viewing much easier.

1. Click on **Using Categories**. The tab will come to the front.

2. Click on a **task(s)** in the task list. The task(s) will be selected.

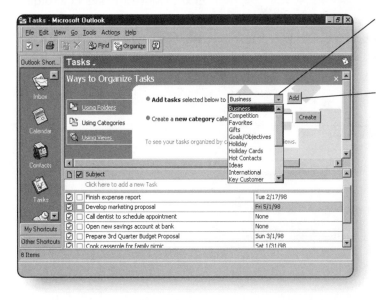

3. Click on the **down arrow** (▼) next to Add and **select** a **category**.

4. Click on **Add**. The category will be added to the selected tasks.

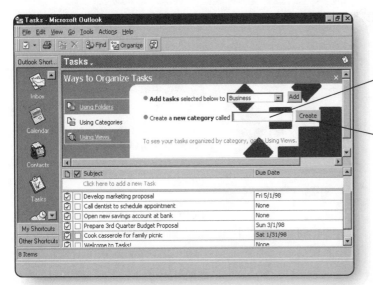

Creating a New Category

1. Type a **new category name** in the Create text box.

2. Click on **Create**. The category will be created.

Once you have created a new category, you can follow the steps from the previous exercise to add the category to selected tasks.

USING VIEWS TO ORGANIZE TASKS

Now that you have explored categories, you may be wondering how they will be used to organize the task list. It's easy! Changing the task list view is one quick way to organize the task list.

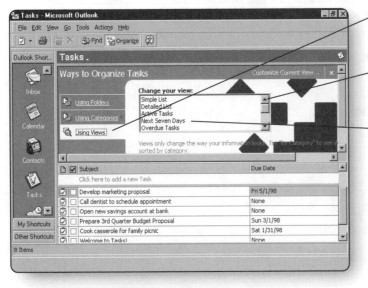

1. Click on **Using Views**. The tab will come to the front.

2. Scroll through the list of views.

3. Click on any **view**. The task list view will change.

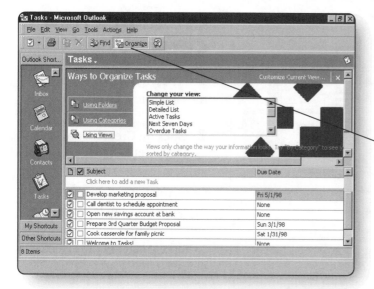

TIP

To view the tasks organized by categories, choose the By Category view.

4. Click on **Organize**. The Ways to Organize Tasks pane will close.

Remember that changing the task view does not delete any existing tasks, it simply removes them from view. To see all tasks, choose the Simple List view.

SORTING THE TASK LIST

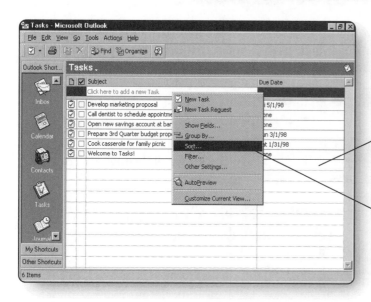

Some people prefer to sort their task lists instead of using views. You can sort by any field in a task, such as priority, due date, or subject.

1. Right-click on a **blank area** of the task list. A shortcut menu will appear.

2. Click on **Sort**. The Sort dialog box will open.

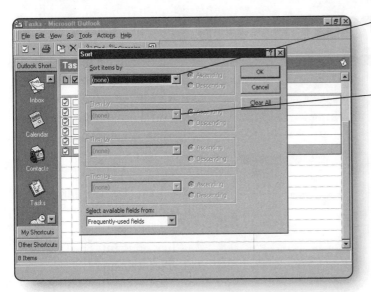

3. Click on the **down arrow** (▼) under Sort items by and **select** a **field** to sort by.

4. Optionally, **click** on the **down arrow** (▼) under Then by and **select** a **field** to sort by for a multiple sort.

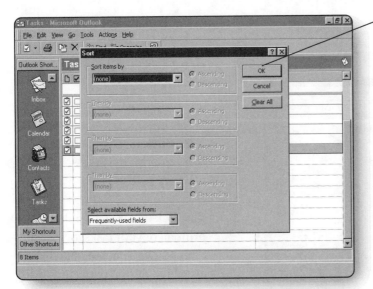

5. Click on **OK**. Your tasks will be sorted according to the criteria you've chosen in steps 3 and 4.

NOTE

If you select a sort field that is not currently displayed on the task list view, a message will open. To add the sort field to the view, click on OK; otherwise, click on No.

PRINTING THE TASK LIST

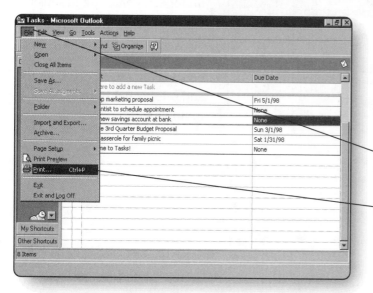

Before attending a meeting or going out of town, you may need to print a list of tasks. Outlook has several options for printing tasks that can give you exactly what you need.

1. **Click** on **File**. The File menu will appear.

2. **Click** on **Print**. The Print dialog box will open.

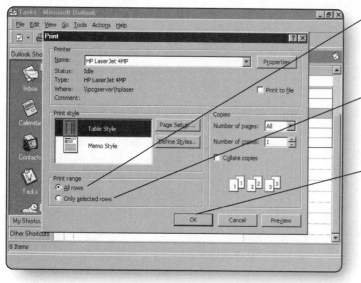

3a. **Click** on **All rows** to print all tasks.

OR

3b. **Click** on **Only selected rows** to print only the selected tasks.

4. **Click** on **OK**. Outlook will print all of your tasks, or just the ones you've selected, depending on which option you chose in step 3.

PART V REVIEW QUESTIONS

1. How do you add a new task? *See "Adding a New Task" in Chapter 19*

2. What should you do if you are afraid of forgetting a task? *See "Setting a Reminder" in Chapter 19*

3. How do you let someone know the status of the task? *See "Sending Status Reports" in Chapter 19*

4. How can you send a task to someone else? *See "Creating a Task Request" in Chapter 20*

5. What are the two ways to reply to a task request? *See "Responding to a Task Request" in Chapter 20*

6. What can you do if you have accepted a task and can't complete it? *See "Declining a Task After You Have Accepted It" in Chapter 20*

7. How can you organize your tasks into folders? *See "Using Folders to Organize Tasks" in Chapter 21*

8. Can you view your task list by category? *See "Using Views to Organize Tasks" in Chapter 21*

9. How do you display sorted tasks? *See "Sorting the Task List" in Chapter 21*

10. Can you print one task or do you have to print the entire Task List? *See "Printing the Task List" in Chapter 21*

PART VI

Tracking Your Time with the Journal

22 Using the Journal

The Journal is a feature that allows you to keep track of all the activities you perform in the course of a day—whether it's responding to a meeting request, sending an e-mail, or opening a document. This feature is essential when billing time to clients or maintaining an accurate record of your daily activities. In this chapter, you'll learn how to:

✦ Automatically track Journal activities

✦ Create a new journal entry

✦ Modify a journal entry

✦ Delete a journal entry

AUTOMATICALLY TRACKING JOURNAL ACTIVITIES

The easiest way to get started with the Journal is to have Outlook automatically record certain types of activities. Some examples of the types of activities you can record are e-mail messages, meeting responses, and task requests.

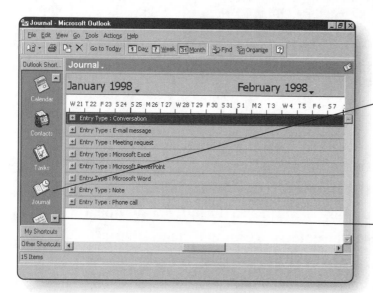

1. Click on the **Journal icon** on the Outlook bar. The Journal will appear in the Information viewer.

NOTE

You may need to click on the scroll arrows on the Outlook bar to see the Journal icon.

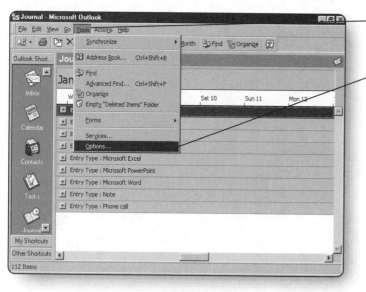

2. Click on **Tools**. The Tools menu will appear.

3. Click on **Options**. The Options dialog box will open.

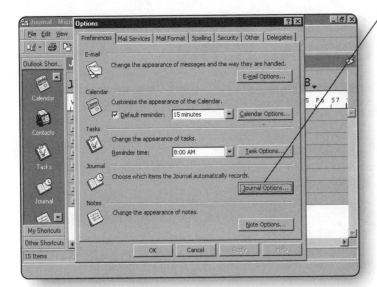

4. **Click** on the **Journal Options button**. The Journal Options dialog box will open.

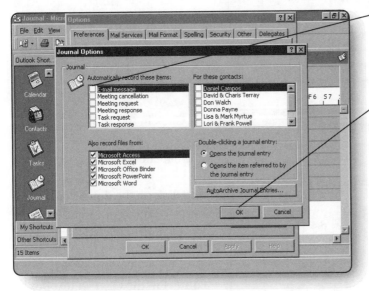

5. **Click** on the **check box** next to the type of items you want to record automatically. A ✔ will be placed in the box.

6. **Click** on **OK** until all open dialog boxes are closed.

CREATING A NEW JOURNAL ENTRY

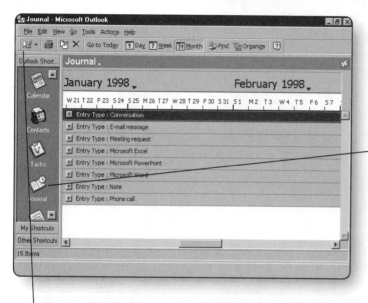

You may have noticed that some activities are not automatically recorded, such as phone calls. Don't worry, there are quick and easy ways to create a journal entry for these activities.

1. Click on the **Journal icon** on the Outlook bar. If you are not already in the Journal, it will appear in the Information viewer. If you are, nothing will happen.

2. Click on the **New Journal button**. The Journal Entry dialog box will open.

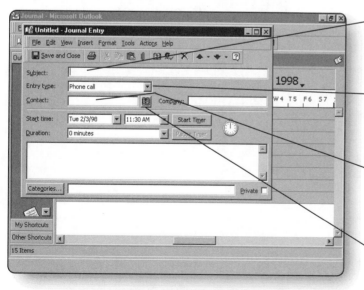

3. Click in the **Subject text box** and **type** the **subject** of the journal entry.

4. Click on the **down arrow (▼)** next to Entry type and **select** the **type** of journal entry.

5a. Type the **name** of the contact in the Contact text box.

OR

5b. Click on the **Address Book button** to access the Address Book or Contact list.

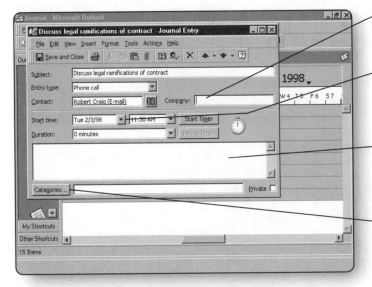

6. Type the **company name** in the Company text box.

7. Click on the **down arrow** (▼) next to Start time to establish the starting time.

8. Click in the **text box** and type any **notes** regarding the journal entry.

9. Click on the **Categories button** and **assign** any **categories** to the contact.

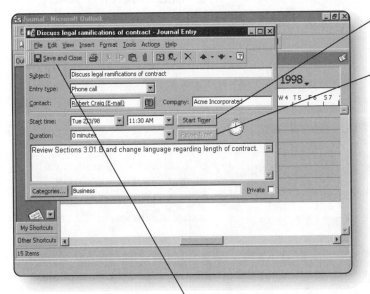

10. Click on the **Start Timer button**. The timer will start.

11. Click on the **Pause Timer button**. The timer will pause.

NOTE

To keep accurate records, pause the timer when you are interrupted or have to temporarily stop recording the activity. Click on the Start Timer button again to resume the timer.

12. Click on the **Save and Close button**. The timer will stop and the journal entry will be saved and closed.

MODIFYING A JOURNAL ENTRY

What happens if you start recording a journal entry and forget to stop the timer when the activity is finished? Don't worry, it's easy to modify journal entries to change inaccurate information, or to add additional information to the entry.

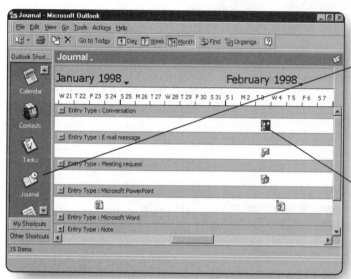

1. **Click** on the **Journal icon** on the Outlook bar. If you are not already in the Journal, it will appear in the Information viewer. If you are, nothing will happen.

2. **Click twice** on any **entry**. The entry will appear.

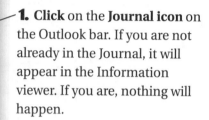

NOTE

To view a single entry, you may need to click on the plus (+) sign to expand the list of entries.

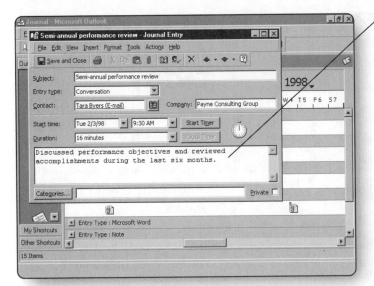

3. Type any **changes** to the entry.

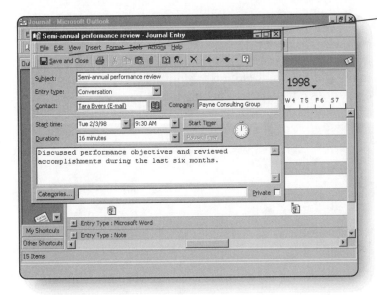

4. Click on the **Save and Close button**. The journal entry will close and any changes you've made will be saved.

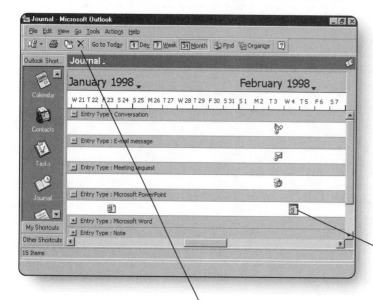

DELETING A JOURNAL ENTRY

When journal entries are automatically recorded, you may end up with some unneeded entries. Deleting a journal entry is very easy with Outlook.

1. **Click** on any **journal entry**. The entry will be selected.

2. **Click** on the **Delete button**. The entry will be deleted.

NOTE

Journal entries are shortcuts that point to the actual item. Deleting the journal entry does not delete the actual item.

23 Changing the Look of the Journal

In the previous chapter, you learned how to create, modify, delete, and automatically track journal entries. Now you can customize your Journal view to make it easier to find and change entries. Also, you'll learn how to tie journal entries to your Contacts and organize journal entries by changing category assignments and view settings. In this chapter, you'll learn how to:

✦ View the Journal

✦ View the journal entries for a contact

✦ Use categories and views to organize the Journal

✦ Customize Journal views

✦ Customize Journal entry actions

VIEWING THE JOURNAL

There are several ways to view the Journal. You can display the entries by type, contact, category, or by looking at the last seven days. In some views, the Journal appears as a timeline— you can scroll through the days to see the recorded activities.

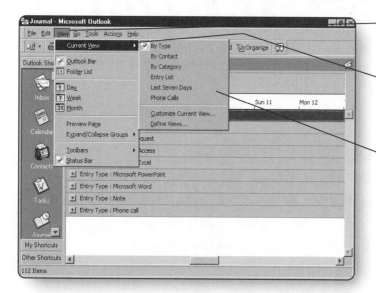

1. Click on **View**. The View menu will appear.

2. Click on **Current View**. The Current View submenu will appear.

3. Click on any **view**. The view will be selected.

If you select the By Type, By Contact, or By Category view, a timeline will appear at the top of the Information viewer.

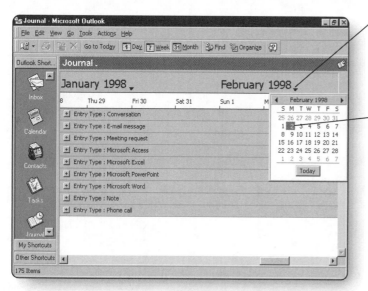

4. Click on the **down arrow** (▼) next to the month name in the banner. A Date Navigator will appear.

5. Click on any **date**. The Journal view will change to focus on the date you've chosen. You can also change views with any of the buttons on the Standard toolbar.

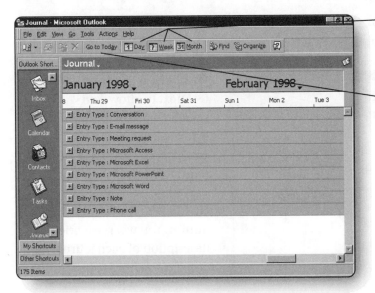

6. **Click** on any of the **View buttons** to switch to day, week, or month view.

7. **Click** on the **Go to Today button** to return to today's date.

VIEWING THE JOURNAL ENTRIES FOR A CONTACT

Outlook also allows you to open a contact record to view all of the activities recorded for the contact. This is a great way to keep track of activities associated with a particular person.

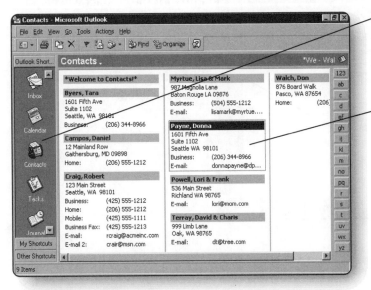

1. **Click** on the **Contacts icon** on the Outlook bar. Your contacts will appear in the Information viewer.

2. **Click twice** on any **contact**. The contact will appear.

3. **Click** on the **Journal tab**. You will see the journal entries for the contact.

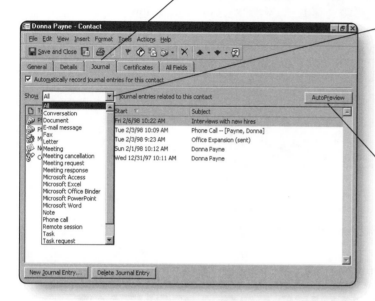

4. **Click** on the **down arrow** (▾) next to Show. You will see specific types of journal entries. If you select an entry type, you can see only that type of journal entry.

5. **Click** on the **AutoPreview button**. You will see a brief description of each journal item.

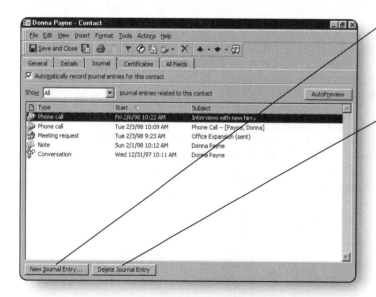

6. **Click** on the **New Journal Entry button**. A new journal entry for the contact will be created.

7. **Click** on the **Delete Journal Entry button**. The journal entry will be deleted.

USING CATEGORIES TO ORGANIZE THE JOURNAL

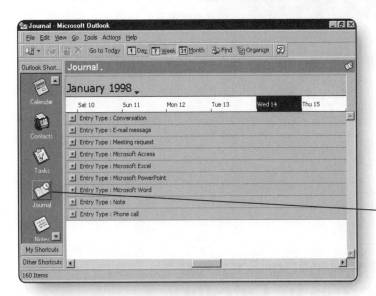

One of the best ways to organize the Journal is by using categories. For example, say you want to add several items to the Key Customer category. Once you have done that, you can view all related activities for Key Customer by viewing journal entries by category.

1. Click on the **Journal icon** on the Outlook bar. Your journal entries will appear in the Information viewer.

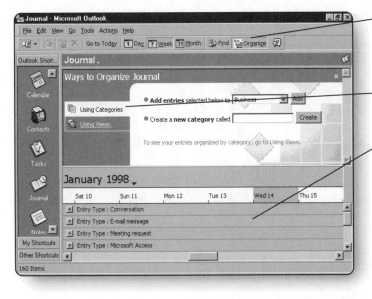

2. Click on the **Organize button**. The Ways to Organize Journal pane will appear.

3. Click on **Using Categories**. The tab will come to the front.

4. Click on any **journal entry**. The entry will be selected.

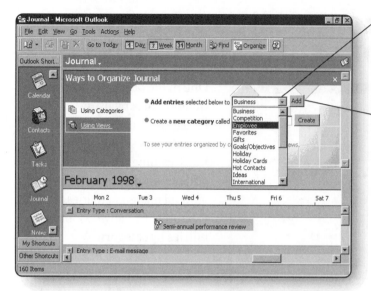

5. Click on the **down arrow (▼)** next to the Add entries selected below to list box and **select** a **category**.

6. Click on the **Add button**. The journal entry will be added to the category selected in step 5.

Displaying Journal Entries by Category

Once the selected items have been added to a category, you can use views to display journal entries by category.

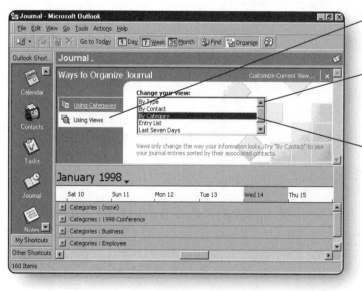

1. Click on **Using Views**. The tab will come to the front.

2. Click on the **scroll arrows** of the Change your view scroll box. The available views will appear.

3. Click on **By Category**. The By Category view will be selected.

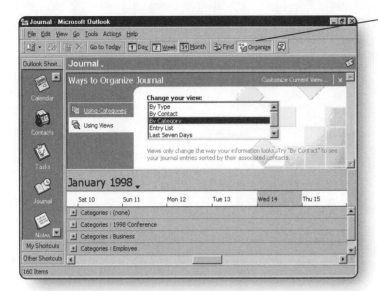

4. Click on the **Organize button**. The Ways to Organize Journal pane will close.

CUSTOMIZING VIEWS

Each of the views in the Journal have pre-defined settings that can easily be changed. Some of the items you can change are including or excluding labels on the journal icons, showing week numbers, or changing the font of the view.

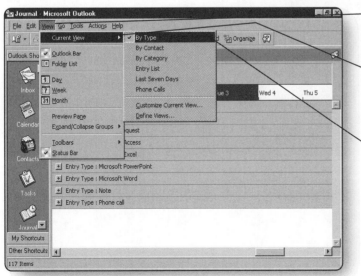

1. Click on **View**. The View menu will appear.

2. Click on **Current View**. The Current View submenu will appear.

3. Click on **By Type, By Contact,** or **By Category**. The Information viewer will change to reflect your selection.

4. Click on **View**. The View menu will appear.

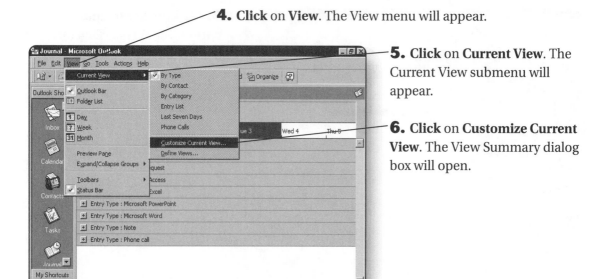

5. Click on **Current View**. The Current View submenu will appear.

6. Click on **Customize Current View**. The View Summary dialog box will open.

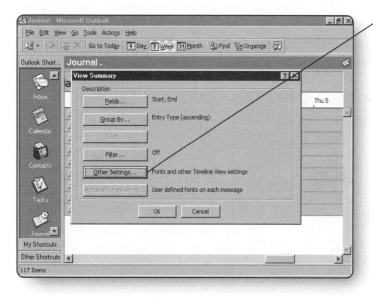

7. Click on the **Other Settings button**. The Format Timeline View dialog box will open.

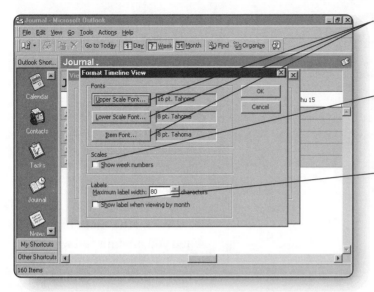

8. **Click** on any of the **buttons** in the Fonts area. The font will change accordingly.

9. **Click** on the **check box** next to Show week numbers. The week numbers will display.

10. **Click** on the **check box** next to Show label when viewing by month. The labels will display.

11. **Click** on **OK** until all open dialog boxes are closed.

CUSTOMIZING JOURNAL ENTRY ACTIONS

When you click twice on a journal entry, one of two things can happen. You can either view the journal entry, or you can view the item associated with the journal entry. For example, clicking twice on an entry of a Word document can open the journal entry or the Word document. There is an advantage to opening the document—you don't have to remember the location, or path, of the document.

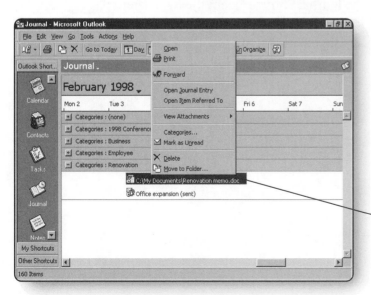

1. **Right-click** on any **journal entry**. A shortcut menu will appear.

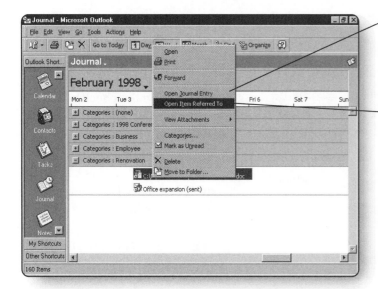

2a. Click on **Open Journal Entry**. The journal entry will appear.

OR

2b. Click on **Open Item Referred To**. The e-mail message, document, spreadsheet, or presentation will open.

3. Click on the **Close button** when you are finished with the item. The item will close.

TIP

You can change the default behavior of Outlook and journal entries. Click on Tools, Options, and then click on Journal Options. In the Double-clicking a Journal Entry section, click on Opens the Journal Entry or Opens the Item Referred to by the Journal Entry.

PART VI REVIEW QUESTIONS

1. Name six types of activities that can be automatically recorded in the Journal. *See "Automatically Tracking Journal Activities" in Chapter 22*

2. How can you manually create a journal entry? *See "Creating a New Journal Entry" in Chapter 22*

3. How can you temporarily stop the timer? *See "Creating a New Journal Entry" in Chapter 22*

4. How do you expand a list of journal entries to see individual entries? *See "Modifying a Journal Entry" in Chapter 22*

5. Does deleting a journal entry delete the item the entry refers to? *See "Deleting a Journal Entry" in Chapter 22*

6. Name three Journal views that display a timeline. *See "Viewing the Journal" in Chapter 23*

7. How would you view all of the phone call entries for a single contact? *See "Viewing the Journal Entries for a Contact" in Chapter 23*

8. How would you add a category to a contact? *See "Using Categories to Organize the Journal" in Chapter 23*

9. How can you view all journal entries by category? *See "Displaying Journal Entries by Category" in Chapter 23*

10. How can you display a label next to the journal entry icons? *See "Customizing Views" in Chapter 23*

PART VII

Capturing Your Thoughts with Notes

24 Creating and Using Notes

The Notes feature in Outlook lets you quickly jot down any important thoughts, reminders, or other information. Use notes in Outlook instead of grabbing the closest scrap of paper around you. In this chapter, you'll learn how to:

✦ Create, edit, and delete a note

✦ Add a category to notes

✦ Turn a note into an e-mail or task

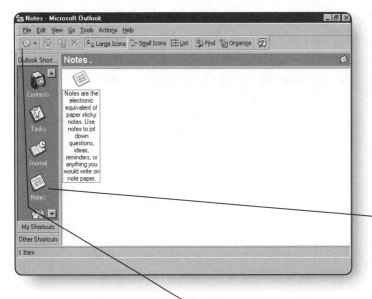

CREATING A NOTE

Creating an electronic note in Outlook is easier than reaching for a pen and paper. Creating notes electronically guarantees that you won't have to transfer them to your computer later on.

1. Click on the **Notes icon** on the Outlook bar. Your notes will appear in the Information viewer.

2. Click on the **New Note button**. A new note window will appear.

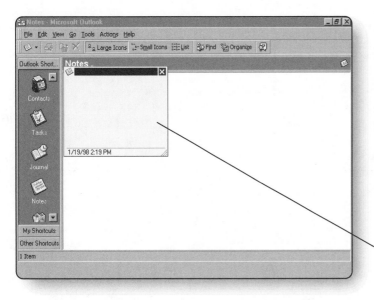

NOTE

If you don't see the date and time at the bottom of the note window, go to the Tools menu and select Options. Select the Other tab and click on the Advanced Options button. From the window that opens, click in the check box labeled "When viewing Notes, show time and date" in the Appearance options section.

3. Type the **note**.

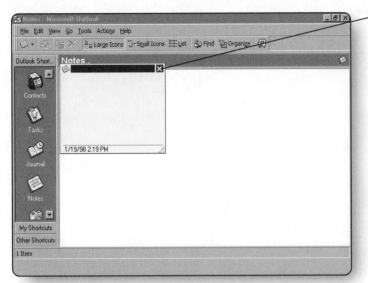

4. **Click** on **Close**. The note will be saved automatically.

TIP

You can press the Esc key to close a note.

NOTE

Only the first paragraph of the note will appear in the note preview in the Information viewer.

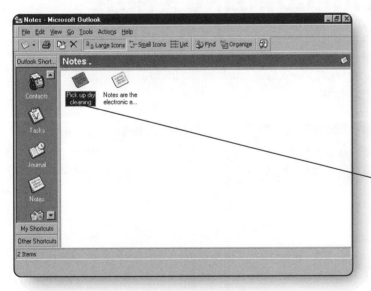

EDITING A NOTE

If you gather more information after creating a note, don't worry—you can update the note even after you have closed it.

1. **Double-click** on any **note icon**. The note will open.

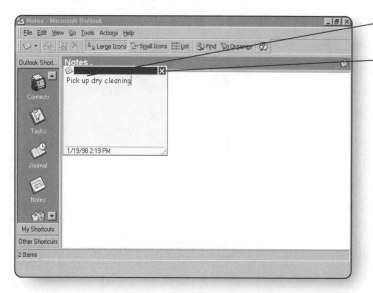

2. Type any **changes**.

3. Click on **Close**. The changes will be saved automatically.

CATEGORIZING A NOTE

It's far easier to organize electronic notes than a stack of phone messages on your desk. You can use Categories in Outlook to group notes into subjects for easy identification and organization.

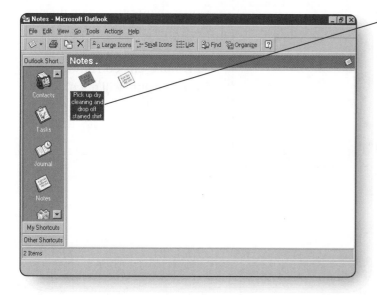

1. **Right-click** on any **note** in the Information viewer. A shortcut menu will appear.

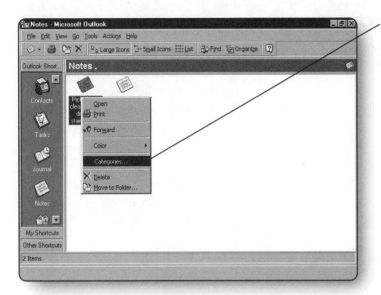

2. Click on **Categories**. The Categories dialog box will open.

3. Click in any **check box** in the Available categories scroll box. A ✔ will be placed in the box.

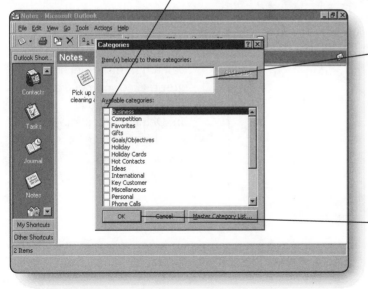

NOTE

Notes can be added to multiple categories, or you can add your own categories. Click in the Item(s) belong to these categories text box, type the name of the new category, and click on the Add to List button.

4. Click on **OK**. Your note will be added to the categories you've selected.

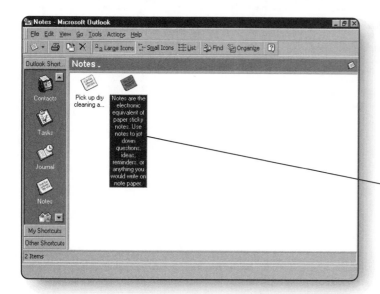

DELETING A NOTE

No longer need your note? Outlook makes it easy to delete notes and keep your desktop clean.

1. Right-click on a **note** in the Information viewer. A shortcut menu will appear.

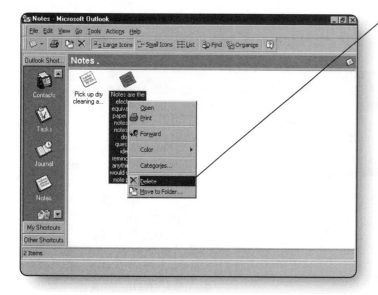

2. Click on **Delete**. The note will be deleted.

NOTE

Deleted notes move to the Deleted Items folder. If you later realize you need a deleted note, you can open the Deleted Items folder and drag the note back to the Notes folder.

TURNING A NOTE INTO ANOTHER OUTLOOK ITEM

Do you want more from your notes? You can send the note content to another person, create a task from the note, or add an item to the calendar by dragging the note into another Outlook folder.

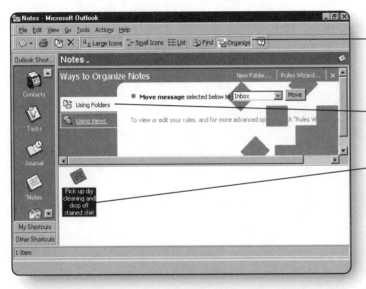

1. **Click** on **Organize**. The Ways to Organize Notes pane will open.

2. **Click** on **Using Folders**. The tab will come to the front.

3. **Click** on any **note** in the note pane. The note will be selected.

TIP

You can select multiple notes by holding down the Ctrl key and clicking on a note.

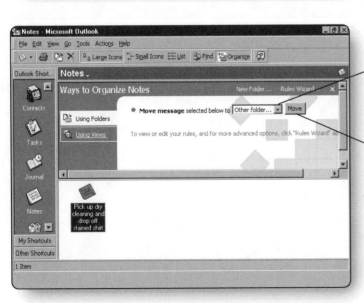

4. **Click** on the **down arrow (▼)** next to Move message selected below to and **select** a **folder**.

5. **Click** on **Move**. The selected note(s) will be moved to a new folder.

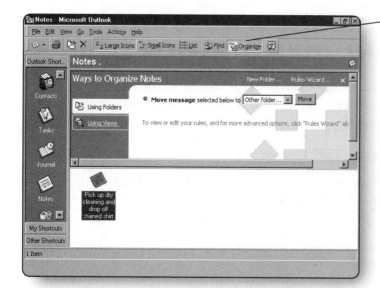

6. Click on **Organize**. The Ways to Organize Notes pane will close.

25 Changing the Look of Notes

The Notes feature in Outlook lets you quickly jot down any important thoughts, reminders, or other information. You can change the appearance of notes to quickly find and identify which note you are looking for. In this chapter, you'll learn how to:

✦ Change note color and displays

✦ Use views to organize notes

✦ Sort or filter views

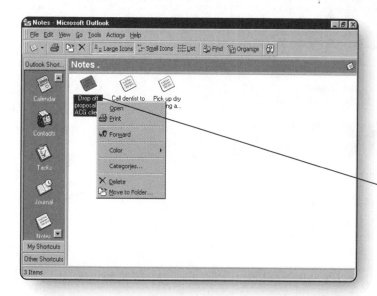

CHANGING NOTE COLORS

If you are visually oriented, Outlook has a great feature that will allow you to organize your notes by color.

1. Right-click on any **note icon**. A shortcut menu will appear.

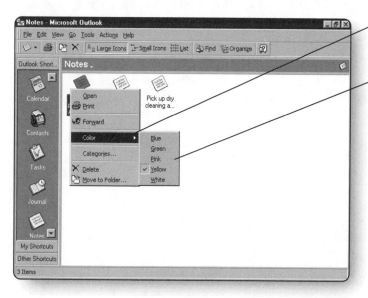

2. Click on **Color**. The Color submenu will appear.

3. Click on any **color**. The color will be applied to the note.

TIP

Colors can be used to organize notes into visual categories. For example, make personal items blue and important items pink. When you apply the color pink to a note, it has the appearance of being red.

Changing Note Defaults

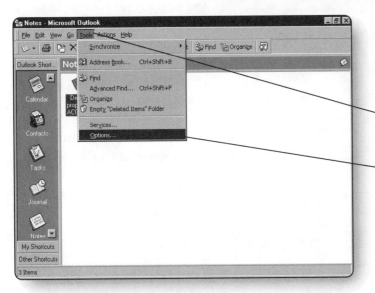

By default, notes are yellow and medium in size. You can change these defaults for any new notes added to the Notes folder.

1. Click on **Tools**. The Tools menu will appear.

2. Click on **Options**. The Options dialog box will open.

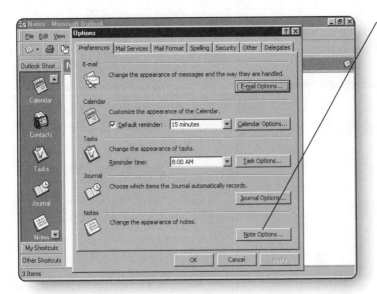

3. Click on the **Note Options button**. The Note Options dialog box will open.

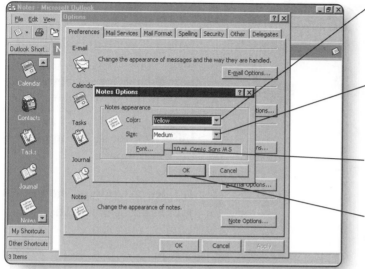

4. Click on the **down arrow** (▼) next to the Color list box and **select** a **color**.

5. Click on the **down arrow** (▼) next to the Size list box and **select** a **size**.

6. Click on the **Font button** and **select** a **font style** and **size**.

7. Click on **OK** until all open dialog boxes are closed.

Changing the Notes Display

Notes are displayed in the Information viewer as icons. You can change the size of the icon or display a simple list of notes instead.

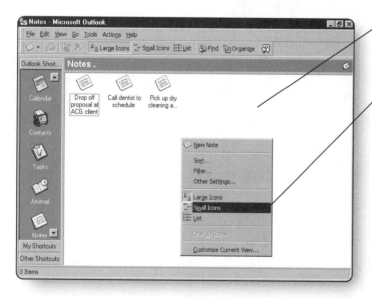

1. Right-click on a **blank area** in the Information viewer. A shortcut menu will appear.

2a. Click on **Small Icons**. Your notes will be displayed as smaller icons. You will be able to see more notes in the Information viewer, but you won't be able to see as much detail on each one.

OR

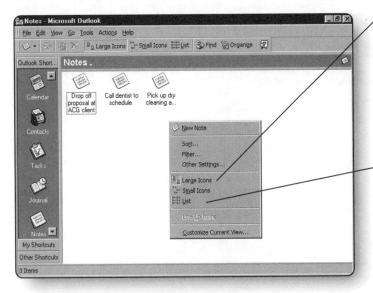

2b. **Click** on **Large Icons**. Your notes will be displayed as larger icons. You won't be able to see as many notes in your Information viewer, but you'll be able to see more details about each one.

OR

2c. **Click** on **List**. Your notes will be visible in a list format.

TIP

There are buttons on the Standard toolbar that let you change the notes display as well.

CHANGING THE NOTES VIEW

Views let you change which notes appear on the screen. Using views is a great way to organize notes or to find the notes you need.

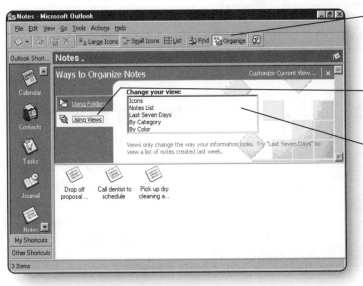

1. **Click** on **Organize**. The Ways to Organize Notes pane will open.

2. **Click** on **Using Views**. The tab will come to the front.

3. **Click** on any **view**. The view will change.

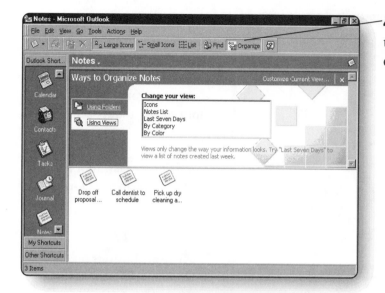

4. Click on **Organize**. The Ways to Organize Notes pane will close.

SORTING AND FILTERING NOTES

Sorting notes groups together similar notes. Once notes have been sorted, you can scroll through all the notes to find the ones you want. Filtering notes allows you to show only the notes you need. The other notes are not deleted; they simply do not display onscreen.

Sorting Notes

1. Right-click on any **blank area** of the Information viewer. A shortcut menu will appear.

2. Click on **Sort**. The Sort dialog box will open.

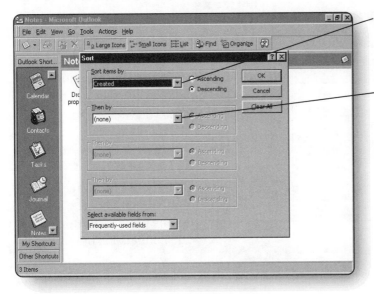

3. **Click** on the **down arrow (▼)** next to Sort items by and **select a sorting criteria**.

4. Optionally, **click** on the **down arrow (▼)** next to Then by to create a second level sort.

5. **Click** on **OK**. Your notes will be sorted according to the options you've selected.

Filtering Notes

Maybe you only want to see a particular type of note. For example, all personal notes, or all notes created on a certain date. Filtering will get to the notes you want without having to see all of the others.

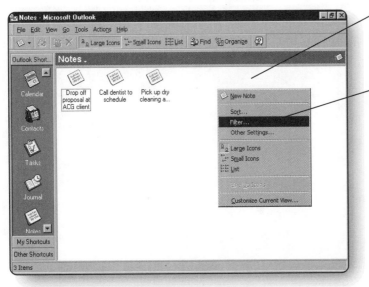

1. **Right-click** on any **blank area** of the Information viewer. A shortcut menu will appear.

2. **Click** on **Filter**. The Filter dialog box will open.

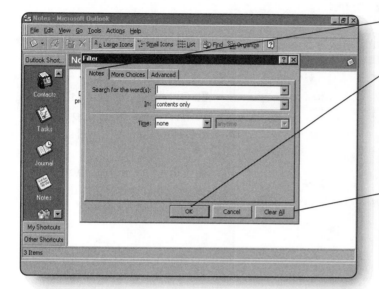

3. Click on any **tab** and **select filter criteria**.

4. Click on **OK**. Your notes will be filtered according to the criteria you've selected.

NOTE

To remove filter criteria and display all notes, click on the Clear All button on the Filter dialog box.

PART VII REVIEW QUESTIONS

1. How do you add a note? *See "Creating a Note" in Chapter 24*

2. How do you edit a note? *See "Editing a Note" in Chapter 24*

3. How do you add a category to a note? *See "Categorizing a Note" in Chapter 24*

4. Where do deleted notes go? *See "Deleting a Note" in Chapter 24*

5. How do you place the contents of a note in an e-mail message? *See "Turning a Note into Another Outlook Item" in Chapter 24*

6. Why would you change the color of a note? *See "Changing Note Colors" in Chapter 25*

7. How can you get notes to appear in a different color, size, or font? *See "Changing Note Defaults" in Chapter 25*

8. Name three display settings for notes. *See "Changing the Notes Display" in Chapter 25*

9. What are the five note views? *See "Changing the Notes View" in Chapter 25*

10. Does applying a filter delete notes or simply change the way the notes look? *See "Filtering Notes" in Chapter 25*

PART VIII

Customizing Your Outlook Environment

26 Accessing Frequently Used Commands

Most Outlook commands appear on the toolbars at the top edge of the screen. If there is a command you use that does not appear on the screen as a toolbar button, don't worry! Outlook allows you to completely customize the toolbars and the Outlook bar, providing you with one-click access to the tasks or folders you need. In this chapter, you'll learn how to:

✦ Add commands to toolbars

✦ Delete commands from toolbars

✦ Reset toolbars

✦ Add groups and shortcuts to the Outlook bar

✦ Add shortcuts to the Outlook bar

ADDING COMMANDS TO TOOLBARS

Do you want to click on a button and have a task you perform often occur? You can add any Outlook command to the toolbars.

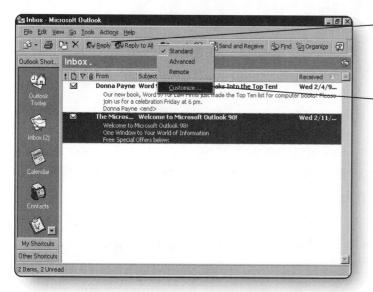

1. Right-click on any **toolbar button**. A shortcut menu will appear.

2. Click on **Customize**. The Customize dialog box will open.

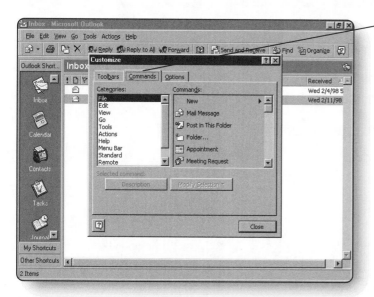

3. Click on the **Commands tab**. The tab will come to the front.

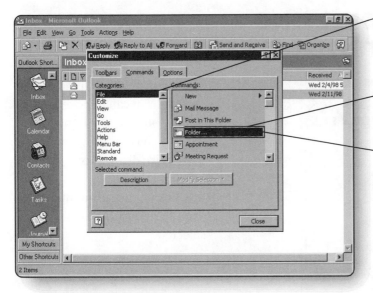

4. Click on any **category**. You will see the commands associated with the category.

5. Click on any **command**. The command will be selected.

6. Click and **drag** the **command** to an existing toolbar. The command will be added.

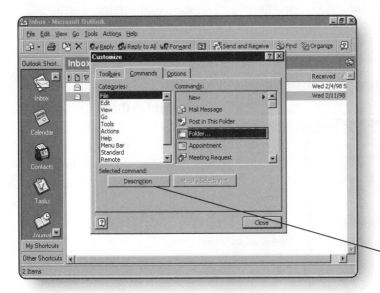

NOTE

As you drag the command, there will be a small X attached to the mouse pointer. When the pointer changes to a plus (+) sign, release the mouse button to place the command on the toolbar.

TIP

Click on a command in the Customize dialog box, and then click on the Description button to see a description of how the command works.

DELETING TOOLBAR BUTTONS

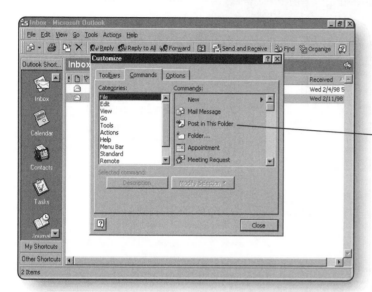

Want a more streamlined toolbar? You can remove any toolbar buttons you don't use on a regular basis through the Customize dialog box.

1. Click on the **command** you want to remove. It will be selected.

NOTE

The Customize dialog box needs to be open to add or delete commands from the toolbars.

2. Click and **drag** the **command** to the Information viewer.

3. Release the **mouse button**. The command will be deleted.

RESETTING TOOLBARS

Whoops! Did you delete a toolbar button by accident? If you've changed a toolbar, Outlook allows you to quickly restore toolbar buttons to their original settings.

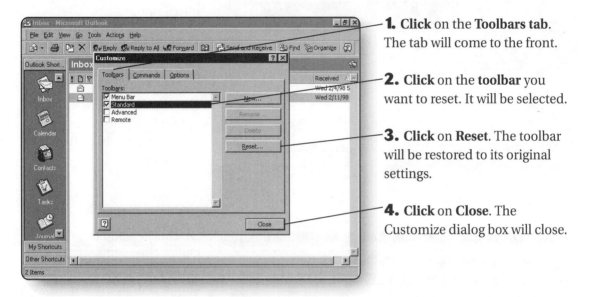

1. **Click** on the **Toolbars tab**. The tab will come to the front.

2. **Click** on the **toolbar** you want to reset. It will be selected.

3. **Click** on **Reset**. The toolbar will be restored to its original settings.

4. **Click** on **Close**. The Customize dialog box will close.

ADDING GROUPS TO THE OUTLOOK BAR

A quick way to access the folders you need is by clicking on the Outlook bar. Folders on the Outlook bar are arranged into groups, and you can add or delete any group on the Outlook bar.

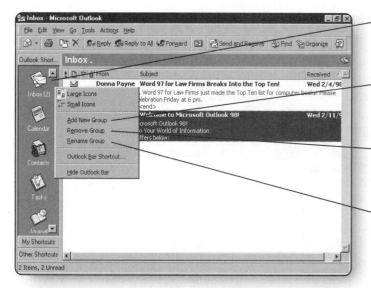

1. Right-click on any **blank area** of the Outlook bar. A shortcut menu will appear.

✦ **Add New Group**. Click on this option to add a new group to the Outlook bar.

✦ **Remove Group**. Click on this option to remove a group from the Outlook bar.

✦ **Rename Group**. Click on this option to rename any group on the Outlook bar with a new name.

NOTE

Deleting a group from the Outlook bar will not remove the folders or their contents from Outlook. The icons on the Outlook bar are shortcuts that point to the actual items.

2. Click in any **blank area**. The shortcut menu will close.

ADDING SHORTCUTS TO THE OUTLOOK BAR

Shortcuts are pointers to the folders you use most frequently. For example, if there is a client folder on the network, you may want to create a shortcut pointing to the folder so you can access the files in it quickly. Once you have a shortcut on the Outlook bar, all you have to do is point and click to navigate to a new location.

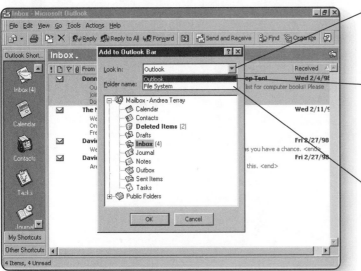

1. Right-click on a **blank area** of the Outlook bar. A shortcut menu will appear.

2. Click on **Outlook Bar Shortcut**. The Add to Outlook Bar dialog box will open.

3. Click on the **down arrow (▼)** next to the Look in list box. Two choices will appear.

4a. Click on **Outlook**. Shortcuts to all Outlook folders will appear.

OR

4b. Click on **File System**. Shortcuts to any folders on your computer or network will appear.

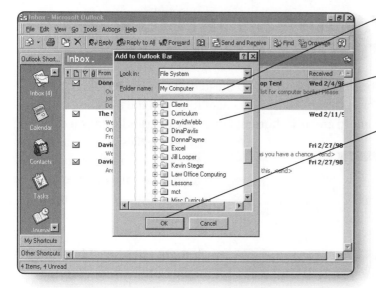

5. Type the **name** of the group in the Folder name list box.

6. Click on the **folder** to which you want to add a shortcut.

7. Click on **OK**. The shortcut will be added.

27 Customizing Your Messages

Are you tired of plain e-mail messages? The white background, the gray headers—maybe it's a little too dull. Don't spend hours trying to spruce up your e-mail messages—let Outlook do it for you! In this chapter, you'll learn how to:

✦ Send mail messages with stationery

✦ Use Microsoft Word as your e-mail editor

SENDING MAIL MESSAGES USING STATIONERY

If you want a new look for your electronic correspondence, you can use stationery to brighten up your messages. But before you can use stationery, Outlook needs to change the format of the e-mail messages to HTML. This is a one-time procedure.

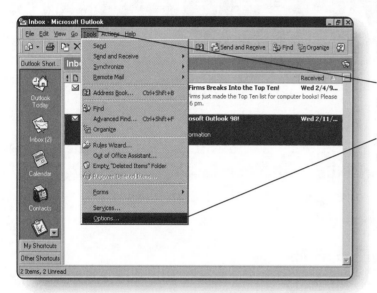

1. **Click** on **Tools**. The Tools menu will appear.

2. **Click** on **Options**. The Options dialog box will open.

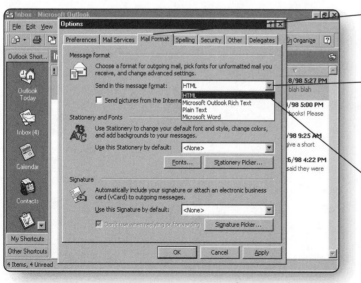

3. **Click** on the **Mail Format tab**. The tab will come to the front.

4. **Click** on the **down arrow (▼)** next to the Send in this message format list box. A drop-down list will appear.

5. **Click** on **HTML**. It will be selected.

Now that Outlook knows you want to use HTML, you can set a default stationery, change the font, or edit the stationery.

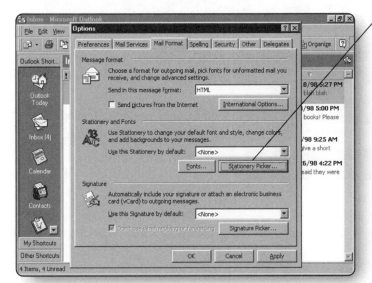

6. Click on **Stationery Picker**. The Stationery Picker dialog box will open.

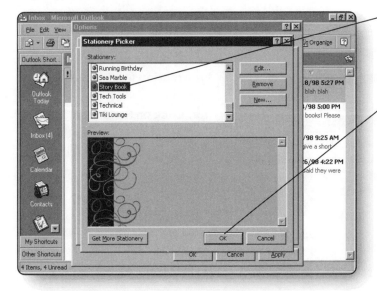

7. Click on any **stationery type** in the Stationery list box. You will see a preview of the stationery.

8. Click on **OK**. The stationery you chose will be the default for all new messages.

9. Click on **File**. The File menu will appear.

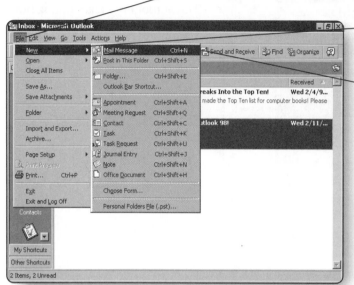

10. Click on **New**. The New submenu will appear.

11. Click on **Mail Message**. A new message will appear, using the default stationery.

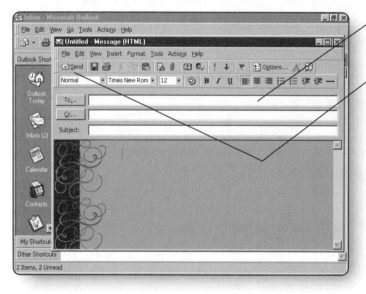

12. Type the **required information** for the message.

13. Click on **Send**. The message will be sent on the stationery you've selected.

Using Other Stationery Patterns

Once you have set a default stationery, you can still use other stationery patterns or send a plain e-mail message.

1. **Click** on the **Inbox icon** on the Outlook bar. Your e-mail messages will appear in the Information viewer.

2. **Click** on **Actions**. The Actions menu will appear.

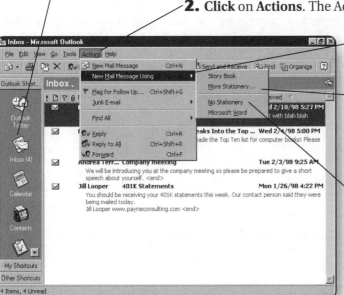

3. **Click** on **New Mail Message Using**. A submenu will appear.

4a. **Click** on **More Stationery.** You will be able to access all of the stationery.

OR

4a. **Click** on **No Stationery.** Your original, default message background will be used.

5. **Click** on **Send** when you're finished addressing and composing the message. The message will be sent with the stationery setting you've chosen.

USING MICROSOFT WORD
AS YOUR E-MAIL EDITOR

If you have used Microsoft Word, you know how many formatting options are available in the application. By using Microsoft Word as your e-mail editor, the full range of formatting options become available to you.

1. Click on **Tools**. The Tools menu will appear.

2. Click on **Options**. The Options dialog box will open.

3. Click on the **Mail Format tab**. The tab will come to the front.

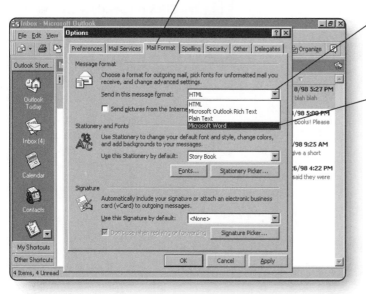

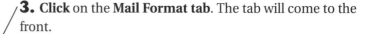

4. Click on the **down arrow (▼)** next to the Send in this message format list box.

5. Click on **Microsoft Word**. It will be selected.

Now that you have designated Microsoft Word as the e-mail editor, you can choose any of the WordMail templates to be used with e-mail.

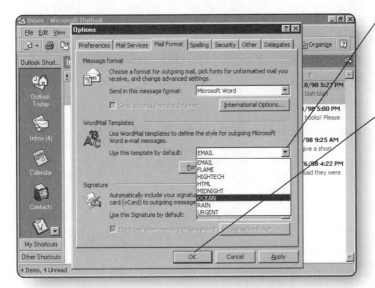

6. Click on the **down arrow (▼)** next to the Use this Template by default list box and **select** any **WordMail template**.

7. Click on **OK**. Microsoft Word will now be your e-mail editor, using the template you selected in step 6.

8. Click on **File**. The File menu will appear.

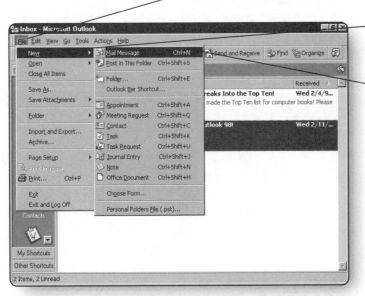

9. Click on **New**. The New submenu will appear.

10. Click on **Mail Message**. A new message will appear, using the default WordMail template.

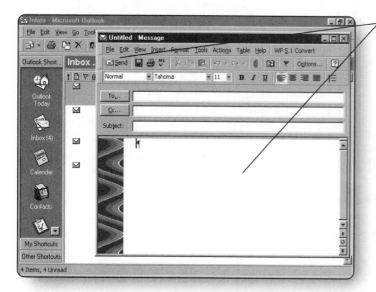

11. **Type** the **required information** for the message and **click** on **Send**. The message will be sent.

NOTE

When you send e-mail using WordMail or stationery, the e-mail recipient must have Outlook in order to see the special formatting.

28 Changing Preferences and Options

One of the most powerful features of Outlook is its ability to adapt to your preferences. If you don't like the way your mail, calendar, or other folders operate, you can easily change your environment. In this chapter, you'll learn how to:

✦ Customize e-mail options

✦ Customize preferences

CUSTOMIZING E-MAIL OPTIONS

You may have noticed that there are numerous default e-mail settings in Outlook. If you don't like the way Outlook e-mail works, you can change it! For example, you can specify what occurs when you close an e-mail message, what occurs when you receive a new e-mail message, and what to do with items in the Deleted Items folder when you exit Outlook.

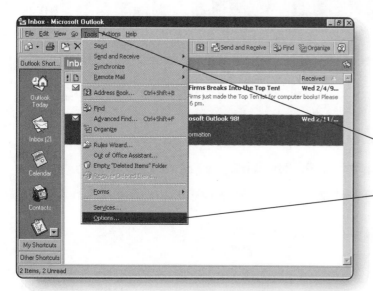

1. **Click** on **Tools**. The Tools menu will appear.

2. **Click** on **Options**. The Options dialog box will open.

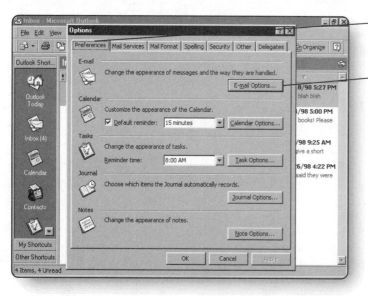

3. **Click** on the **Preferences tab**. The tab will come to the front.

4. **Click** on the **E-mail Options button**. The E-mail Options dialog box will open.

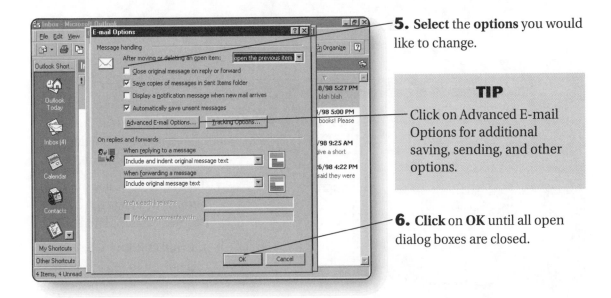

5. **Select** the **options** you would like to change.

6. **Click** on **OK** until all open dialog boxes are closed.

CUSTOMIZING PREFERENCES

The Inbox is not the only folder you can customize in your Outlook environment. The Calendar, Notes, Journal, and Tasks can all be tailored to fit your needs.

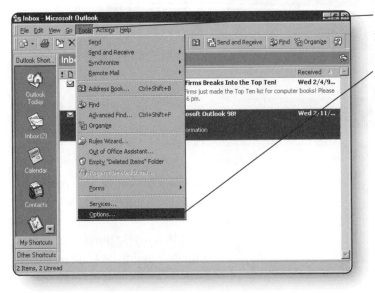

1. **Click** on **Tools**. The Tools menu will appear.

2. **Click** on **Options**. The Options dialog box will open.

3. **Click** on the **Preferences tab**. The tab will come to the front.

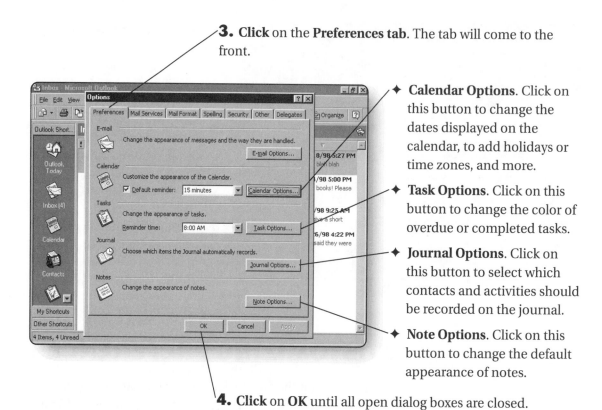

✦ **Calendar Options**. Click on this button to change the dates displayed on the calendar, to add holidays or time zones, and more.

✦ **Task Options**. Click on this button to change the color of overdue or completed tasks.

✦ **Journal Options**. Click on this button to select which contacts and activities should be recorded on the journal.

✦ **Note Options**. Click on this button to change the default appearance of notes.

4. **Click** on **OK** until all open dialog boxes are closed.

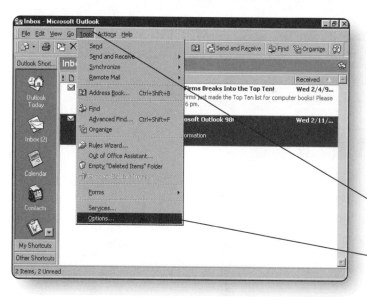

Changing Additional Preferences

Still don't have exactly what you want? There are some additional preferences you can change in Outlook.

1. **Click** on **Tools**. The Tools menu will appear.

2. **Click** on **Options**. The Options dialog box will open.

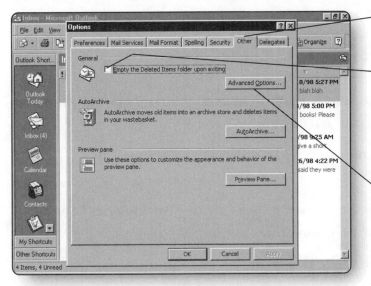

3. Click on the **Other tab**. The tab will come to the front.

4. Click on the **check box** next to Empty the Deleted Items folder upon exiting. The deleted items will be emptied every time you exit the program.

5. Click on the **Advanced Options button**. The Advanced Options dialog box will open.

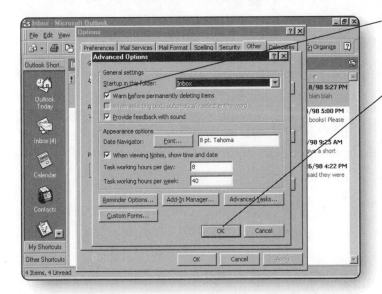

6. Click on the **check box** next to the options you want to select.

7. Click on **OK** until all open dialog boxes are closed.

PART VIII REVIEW QUESTIONS

1. How do you add a command button to your toolbar? *See "Adding Commands to Toolbars" in Chapter 26*

2. How do you reset your toolbar? *See "Resetting Toolbars" in Chapter 26*

3. How do you add a new group of folders to your Outlook bar? *See "Adding Groups to the Outlook Bar" in Chapter 26*

4. How do you add a shortcut to a group on your Outlook bar? *See "Adding Shortcuts to the Outlook Bar" in Chapter 26*

5. In order to use stationery for messages, what format must your e-mail messages be in? *See "Sending Mail Messages Using Stationery" in Chapter 27*

6. How do you set a default stationery? *"Sending Mail Messages Using Stationery" in Chapter 27*

7. If you have default stationery set, how do you choose no stationery for a single message? *See "Using Other Stationery Patterns" in Chapter 27*

8. Where do you set the option to receive a notification when a new e-mail message arrives? *See "Customizing E-mail Options" in Chapter 28*

9. How do you add holidays to your calendar? *See "Customizing Preferences" in Chapter 28*

10. How do you make Outlook empty your Deleted Items folder upon exiting? *See "Changing Additional Preferences" in Chapter 28*

PART IX

Appendix

A Installing Outlook 98

Unless you are working at a computer that already has Outlook 98 installed, you will need to install the application. In this chapter, you'll learn how to:

✦ Install Outlook 98

INSTALLING OUTLOOK 98

To start installing Outlook 98, first place the CD in the CD-ROM drive of the computer. If Outlook 98 is located on a network, you can connect to the network and find the location of the program.

It's a good idea to exit any programs that are currently running on your computer, such as word processing software, spreadsheet software, or e-mail, before you attempt to install any application. Outlook will restart your computer when the installation is complete, and you don't want to lose any of your work.

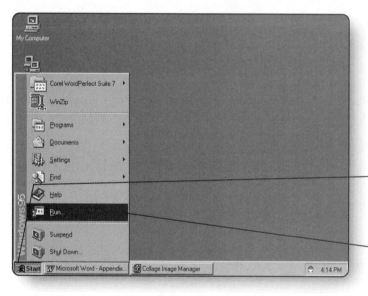

NOTE

Some computers may automatically start running the Setup program on the CD. If so, you can skip to ahead to step 8.

1. **Click** on the Windows 95 or Windows NT **Start button**. The Start menu will appear.

2. **Click** on **Run**. The Run dialog box will open.

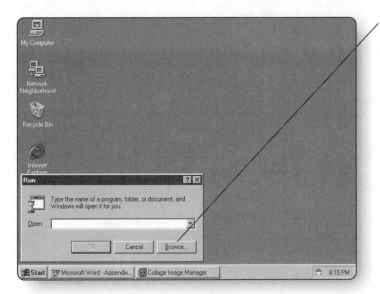

3. **Click** on **Browse**. The Browse dialog box will open.

4. **Click** on the **down arrow** (▼) next to the Look in list box and **navigate** to the **CD-ROM drive**.

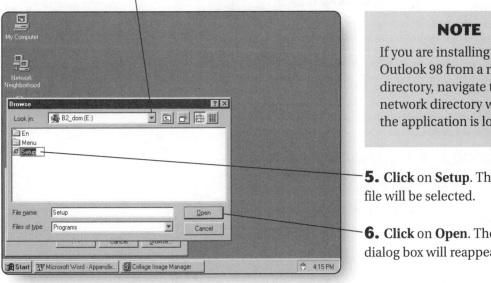

NOTE

If you are installing Outlook 98 from a network directory, navigate to the network directory where the application is located.

5. **Click** on **Setup**. The Setup file will be selected.

6. **Click** on **Open**. The Run dialog box will reappear.

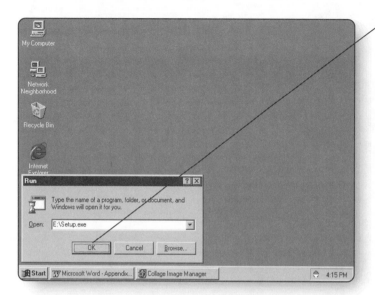

7. Click on **OK**. The Outlook 98 Active Setup will begin.

> ### NOTE
> My computer's CD-ROM drive is named E:, which is why the figure displays E:\SETUP.EXE. Your computer may use another drive, such as the D: drive.

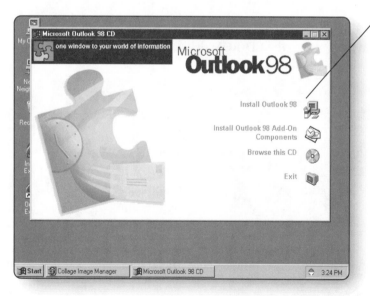

8. Click on **Install Outlook 98**. The Outlook 98 Active Setup will begin.

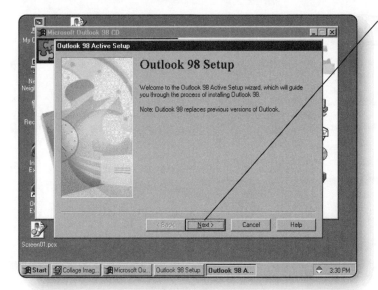

9. Click on **Next**. The Registration dialog box will open.

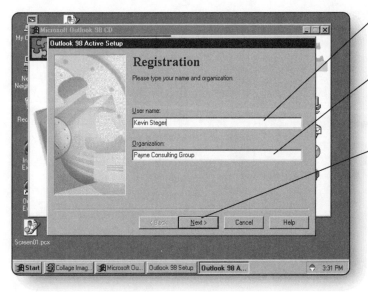

10. Type your **name** in the User name text box.

11. Type the **name of your organization** in the Organization text box.

12. Click on **Next**. The Installation Options dialog box will open.

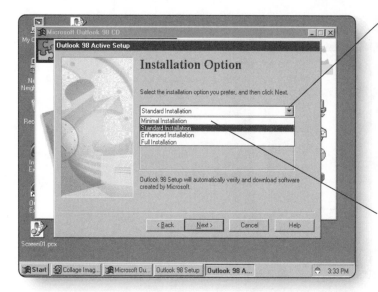

13. **Click** on the **down arrow** (▼) and **select** the **type of installation** you want.

Outlook 98 has four types of available installations. Depending on which installation type you choose, different options will be available in the application.

✦ **Minimal Installation**. Click on Minimal Installation to install Outlook 98 and Internet Explorer 4.0 Web Browser.

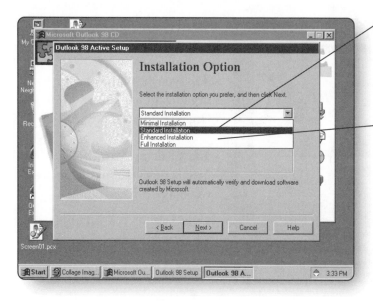

✦ **Standard Installation**. Click on Standard Installation to install Outlook 98, Internet Explorer 4.0 Web Browser, and Outlook Help.

✦ **Enhanced Installation**. Click on Enhanced Installation to install Outlook 98, Internet Explorer 4.0 Web Browser, Outlook Help, Office Assistants, PIM Converters, and System Tools.

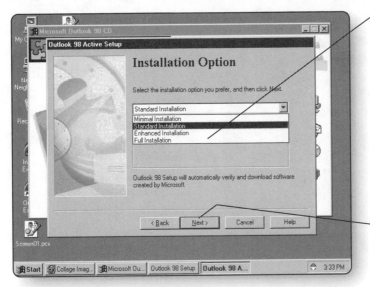

✦ **Full Installation**. Click on Full Installation to install Outlook 98, Internet Explorer 4.0 Web Browser, Outlook Help, Office Assistants, PIM Converters, System Tools, Database Converters, Development Tools, and additional Outlook Enhancements.

14. **Click** on **Next.** The E-mail Upgrade Options dialog box will open.

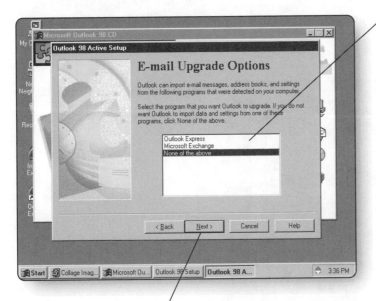

15. **Click** on any **Upgrade option**. Upgrade options will allow Outlook 98 to upgrade existing e-mail programs on your computer.

NOTE

This dialog box will not display unless you have an existing e-mail program installed on your computer.

16. **Click** on N**ext**. The E-mail Service Options dialog box will open.

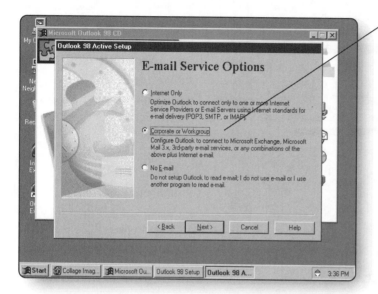

17. Click on **one** of the **E-mail Service Options**. The option will be selected.

NOTE

If you choose the Internet Only version of Outlook 98, some of the features discussed in this book may not be installed.

TIP

Even if you are working at home and are not connected to a corporate e-mail system, you can select the Corporate or Workgroup option.

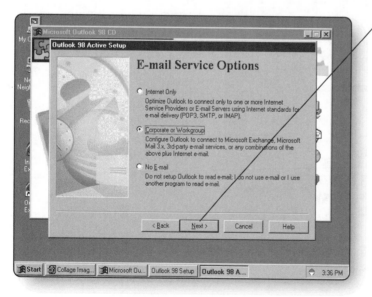

18. Click on **Next.** The Install in folder dialog box will open.

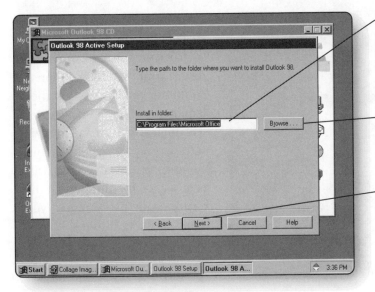

19a. **Type** the **path** to the folder in which you want to install Outlook 98.

OR

19b. **Click** on **Browse** to navigate to the folder in which you want to install Outlook 98.

20. **Click** on **Next**. The Preparing Setup dialog box will open.

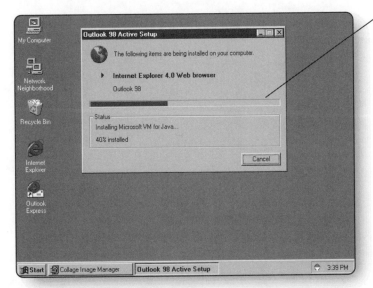

After a few moments, the Active Setup window will appear. This will remain onscreen while Outlook is installing. You can monitor the progress of the installation in the Status area of the window. If you need to cancel the installation for any reason, click on the Cancel button.

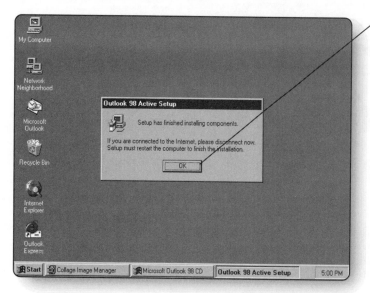

Congratulations! You have successfully installed Outlook 98. Click on OK and Outlook will restart your computer. When the computer restarts, the Internet Explorer 4.0 Setup dialog box will open and begin customizing settings on your machine. This is a one-time procedure and will take several minutes. When the customization is complete, you can start using Outlook 98.

Glossary

A

Address Book. An electronic file that allows you to store e-mail addresses and other information. An address book may be global or personal.

Address Map. A way to view the location of an address on a map via the Internet.

Adult Content Mail. Mail that would not be suitable for individuals under the age of 18.

Appointment. A scheduled block of time on the calendar. Appointments can contain information about the purpose, location, and duration of the engagement.

Archive. A process of retrieving dated information and placing it into another location. Archived information is still available; it is simply located in another folder.

Attachment. A document or file that is a part of an e-mail message.

AutoPreview. An Inbox view that allows you to display the first three lines of text in the e-mail message.

AutoArchive. A process of automatically retrieving dated information and placing it into another folder. AutoArchiving will reduce the size of the folders and keep Outlook operating optimally. By default, Outlook will prompt you to AutoArchive items older than 14 days.

Automatic Signature. A way to include your name and other information automatically at the bottom of every e-mail message.

AutoPick. AutoPick allows Outlook to search for a mutually available meeting time for all meeting attendees.

B

Bullets. Symbols that precede an item in a list.

C

Calendar. An Outlook folder that displays meetings, appointments, and events.

Categories. Words or phrases used to group together similar Outlook items.

Certificates. Companion files that contain digital identification codes (also known as Digital IDs).

Contacts. An electronic Rolodex. May include information such as addresses, phone numbers, e-mail addresses, and Web pages.

Current View. An option on the View menu that allows you to control the display of items on the screen. You can choose one of Outlook's standard views, or you can design your own.

D

Date Navigator. A thumbnail picture of a month. The Date Navigator is a quick way to change the day, week, or month displayed on the screen.

Desktop. When you start your computer, the large area on your screen is called the desktop.

Dialog Box. A box that appears onscreen and presents settings that can be selected and activated.

Directory Server. The server that hosts your online meeting. An example is uls.microsoft.com.

Draft Message. A message that has not yet been sent. If you don't have time to complete a message and would like to return to it, saving the message will place it in the Drafts folder for later retrieval.

E

E-mail Address. A unique identifier that allows others to deliver electronic messages. An individual may have more than one e-mail address. An example is elvis@graceland.com.

E-mail Editor. The interface used to compose e-mail messages.

Event. Any appointment that lasts longer than 24 hours.

Exchange Server. A computer that processes messages and other Outlook items. Think of it as your electronic post office.

Extended Menus. A menu command that has a right-pointing arrow. When you click on an extended menu, another menu appears next to it.

F

Field. A space in which information is entered. Some examples of fields in e-mail messages are Subject and Date Received.

Filter. A filter excludes certain types of items. For example, you can filter your e-mail to include only those received in the last seven days.

Flag. Use a flag to mark an item for special attention. For example, a flag can indicate that an item needs further review.

Folder. In Outlook, folders store items. Folders include the Inbox, Calendar, Tasks, Contacts, Journal, and Notes.

Forward. When you receive an e-mail message that you think others would like to read, but they are not on the original distribution list, you can click on Forward to send it to them.

G

Global Address List. A place to keep addresses that can be accessed by many people.

Groups. A set of items (messages, tasks, and so on) with a common element, such as messages of high priority or contacts from the same company. Groups can be sorted, expanded, and collapsed.

H

HTML. HyperText Markup Language. Used for composing e-mail messages with stationery.

I

Icon. A picture that represents a command or folder.

Inbox. The Inbox stores all of your incoming e-mail messages.

Information viewer. The display area for e-mail messages, calendar items, contacts, tasks, journal items, or notes.

J

Journal. The Journal is an Outlook folder that stores records of phone calls, meetings, meeting responses, and other activities.

Journal Entry. An individual record of a single activity, such as a phone call.

Junk Mail. Unsolicited e-mail.

M

Menu Commands. Options that appear on the menu bar that will perform a function.

Message Recall. A method for retrieving an e-mail message from the recipient's Inbox before they are able to read the item.

Microsoft NetMeeting. Free, downloadable software from Microsoft that allows you to conduct an online meeting.

Microsoft Office. A suite of software applications from Microsoft Corporation. It includes Word, Outlook, Excel, PowerPoint, and Access.

N

Navigate. A way to locate and select a computer directory or date.

Notes. An Outlook folder that allows you to post ideas, thoughts, or quick bits of information on electronic sticky notes.

O

Office Assistant. A Help system from Microsoft that allows you to ask questions and receive answers regarding Outlook.

Online Meeting. A method of communicating with others simultaneously across the Internet. Online meetings can contain typed discussions, real-time video, and spoken conversation.

Online Meeting Request. The command used to invite other individuals to an online meeting and to give them the information they need to join the meeting.

Organize. An Outlook feature that presents different ways of arranging items in the Information viewer.

Outbox. An Outlook folder in which outgoing e-mail messages are stored. This is a temporary holding bin; once the items are sent, they are moved from the Outbox to the Sent Items folder.

Outlook Bar. The gray column on the left of the screen that contains shortcuts to the Outlook folders.

Outlook Today. A snapshot preview of the day's activities, e-mail messages, and tasks.

P

PDL. Personal Distribution List. A PDL is a list of e-mail addresses that you create and maintain. The name of the PDL can be entered on the To line of a message, instead of typing each individual address.

Personal Address Book. A storage location for personal e-mail addresses—sometimes referred to as a PAB file.

Personal Distribution List. See PDL.

Plan a Meeting. An option that allows you to review the meeting attendees' schedules before requesting a meeting time.

Preview Pane. A preview of each item in the folder. The preview allows you to see most of the item without opening it.

Print Style. The print style consists of the pre-defined font, page setup, and header and footer settings for a print job. You can create new print styles or modify existing ones.

Profile. A setting that tells Outlook who you are. Profiles allow more than one person to access Outlook at each computer.

Properties. Settings assigned to each folder that determine permissions, synchronization, and more. Properties are accessed by right-clicking on a folder in the Outlook bar.

R

Recurring Appointment. An appointment that occurs more than once, such as a daily, weekly, or monthly meeting.

Reminder. An electronic update that will notify you a certain time before an appointment, meeting, or task due date.

Reply. An electronic response to the sender of an e-mail message.

Reply to All. An electronic response to the sender and all other recipients of an e-mail message.

Resource. A resource can be a conference room or a piece of audiovisual equipment. Resources appear in the Location box in the Meeting Request.

Right Mouse Click. Moving the mouse pointer over an item and clicking the button located on the right side of the mouse to display a shortcut menu. Sometimes referred to as an alternate click.

Rules Wizard. A step-by-step guide for creating rules that manage your incoming messages.

S

ScreenTip. A box that pops up on the screen when the mouse pointer is held over a toolbar button.

Scroll. The action of clicking on scroll arrows on a list box to display more of the item on the screen.

Scroll bar. The horizontal or vertical bar used to navigate through numerous items. Clicking on the scroll arrows, or clicking and dragging the box on the scroll bar, will change the items displayed.

Sensitivity. A level of privacy attached to a mail item. Items can be set to Normal, Personal, Private, or Confidential sensitivity.

Sent Items Folder. An Outlook folder that contains all sent items, such as e-mail messages, meeting requests, and task requests.

Shortcut. A pointer to an item or folder that provides one-click access. Deleting a shortcut does not delete the actual item or folder.

Snooze. Temporarily suspending a reminder. Similar to a snooze button on an alarm clock.

Sort. A method of displaying items in a certain order in the Information viewer.

Start Page. The default display of Outlook when the application is started. Any Outlook folder, including Outlook Today, can be set as a start page.

Stationery. A background for e-mail messages.

Stationery Picker. A method for choosing or designing stationery.

Status Report. An update on the progress of a task.

T

Task Request. A task sent to another person. An individual receiving a task request can accept, tentatively accept, or decline the task.

Tasks. An Outlook folder that contains items in your task list. Tasks are useful for recording a to-do list and prioritizing assignments.

Toolbar. A bar at the top of the screen that contains Outlook commands. Toolbars can display toolbar buttons or drop-down menus. Outlook toolbars can be customized.

Toolbar Button. A button on a toolbar allows one-click access to perform a command.

Tracking Options. A method for tracing the progress of an item as it is sent and read by the recipient.

V

View. The display for the Information viewer. The view can be changed to any of several other Outlook views, or new views can be created.

W

Web Page Address. The location of a Web page, usually starting with http://www.

Index

Send Us
YOUR COMMENTS

Dear Reader:

Thank you for buying this book. In order to offer you more quality books on the topics *you* would like to see, we need your input. At Prima Publishing, we pride ourselves on timely responsiveness to our readers needs. If you'll complete and return this brief questionnaire, *we will listen!*

Name: (first) _____ (M.I.) _____ (last) _____

Company: _____ Type of business: _____

Address: _____ City: _____ State: _____ Zip: _____

Phone: _____ Fax: _____ E-mail address: _____

May we contact you for research purposes? ❏ Yes ❏ No

(If you participate in a research project, we will supply you with your choice of a book from Prima CPD)

❶ How would you rate this book, overall?

❏ Excellent ❏ Fair
❏ Very Good ❏ Below Average
❏ Good ❏ Poor

❷ Why did you buy this book?

❏ Price of book ❏ Content
❏ Author's reputation ❏ Prima's reputation
❏ CD-ROM/disk included with book
❏ Information highlighted on cover
❏ Other (Please specify): _____

❸ How did you discover this book?

❏ Found it on bookstore shelf
❏ Saw it in Prima Publishing catalog
❏ Recommended by store personnel
❏ Recommended by friend or colleague
❏ Saw an advertisement in: _____
❏ Read book review in: _____
❏ Saw it on Web site: _____
❏ Other (Please specify): _____

❹ Where did you buy this book?

❏ Bookstore (name)_____
❏ Computer Store (name) _____
❏ Electronics Store (name) _____
❏ Wholesale Club (name) _____
❏ Mail Order (name) _____
❏ Direct from Prima Publishing
❏ Other (please specify): _____

❺ Which computer periodicals do you read regularly? _____
_____
_____
_____

❻ Would you like to see your name in print?

May we use your name and quote you in future Prima Publishing books or promotional materials?

❏ Yes ❏ No

❼ Comments & Suggestions: _____
_____
_____

SAVE A STAMP

Visit our Web Site at **www.primapublishing.com**
and simply fill in one of our online Response Forms

11 I would be interested in computer books on these topics

☐ Word Processing ☐ Database:
☐ Networking ☐ Spreadsheets
☐ Desktop Publishing ☐ Web site design
Other _____

9 How do you rate your level of computer skills?

☐ Beginner
☐ Advanced
☐ Intermediate

10 What is your age?

☐ Under 18
☐ 18-24 ☐ 40-49
☐ 25-29 ☐ 50-59
☐ 30-39 ☐ 60-over

8 Where do you use your computer?

Work ☐ 100% ☐ 75% ☐ 50% ☐ 25%
Home ☐ 100% ☐ 75% ☐ 50% ☐ 25%
School ☐ 100% ☐ 75% ☐ 50% ☐ 25%
Other _____

PLEASE
PLACE
STAMP
HERE

PRIMA PUBLISHING

Computers & Technology
3875 Atherton Road
Rocklin, CA 95765

OTHER BOOKS FROM PRIMA PUBLISHING
Computers & Technology

ISBN	Title	Price
0-7615-1363-9	Access 97 Fast & Easy	$16.99
0-7615-1175-X	ACT! 3.0 Fast & Easy	$16.99
0-7615-1348-5	Create FrontPage 98 Web Pages In a Weekend	$24.99
0-7615-1294-2	Create PowerPoint Presentations In a Weekend	$19.99
0-7615-0692-6	Create Your First Web Page In a Weekend	$24.99
0-7615-0428-1	The Essential Excel 97 Book	$27.99
0-7615-0733-7	The Essential Netscape Communicator Book	$24.99
0-7615-0969-0	The Essential Office 97 Book	$27.99
0-7615-0695-0	The Essential Photoshop Book	$35.00
0-7615-1182-2	The Essential PowerPoint 97 Book	$24.99
0-7615-1136-9	The Essential Publisher 97 Book	$24.99
0-7615-0752-3	The Essential Windows NT 4 Book	$27.99
0-7615-0427-3	The Essential Word 97 Book	$27.99
0-7615-0425-7	The Essential WordPerfect 8 Book	$24.99
0-7615-1008-7	Excel 97 Fast & Easy	$16.99
0-7615-1194-6	Increase Your Web Traffic In a Weekend	$19.99
0-7615-1191-1	Internet Explorer 4.0 Fast & Easy	$19.99
0-7615-1137-7	Jazz Up Your Web Site In a Weekend	$24.99
0-7615-1379-5	Learn Access 97 In a Weekend	$19.99
0-7615-1293-4	Learn HTML In a Weekend	$24.99
0-7615-1295-0	Learn the Internet In a Weekend	$19.99
0-7615-1217-9	Learn Publisher 97 In a Weekend	$19.99
0-7615-1251-9	Learn Word 97 In a Weekend	$19.99
0-7615-1193-8	Lotus 1-2-3 97 Fast & Easy	$16.99
0-7615-1420-1	Managing with Microsoft Project 98	$29.99
0-7615-1382-5	Netscape Navigator 4.0 Fast & Easy	$16.99
0-7615-1162-8	Office 97 Fast & Easy	$16.99
0-7615-1186-5	Organize Your Finances with Quicken Deluxe 98 In a Weekend	$19.99
0-7615-1513-5	Publisher 98 Fast & Easy	$19.99
0-7615-1192-X	SmartSuite 97 Fast & Easy	$16.99
0-7615-1138-5	Upgrade Your PC In a Weekend	$19.99
1-55958-738-5	Windows 95 Fast & Easy	$19.95
0-7615-1007-9	Word 97 Fast & Easy	$16.99
0-7615-1316-7	Word 97 for Law Firms	$29.99
0-7615-1083-4	WordPerfect 8 Fast & Easy	$16.99
0-7615-1188-1	WordPerfect Suite 8 Fast & Easy	$16.99

TO ORDER BOOKS

Please send me the following items:

Quantity	Title	Unit Price	Total
_____	_____	$_____	$_____
_____	_____	$_____	$_____
_____	_____	$_____	$_____
_____	_____	$_____	$_____
_____	_____	$_____	$_____
	Subtotal		$_____
	Deduct 10% when ordering 3–5 books		$_____
	7.25% Sales Tax (CA only)		$_____
	8.25% Sales Tax (TN only)		$_____
	5.0% Sales Tax (MD and IN only)		$_____
	Shipping and Handling*		$_____
	TOTAL ORDER		$_____

Shipping and Handling depend on Subtotal.

Subtotal	Shipping/Handling
$0.00–$14.99	$3.00
$15.00–29.99	$4.00
$30.00–49.99	$6.00
$50.00–99.99	$10.00
$100.00–199.99	$13.00
$200.00+	call for quote

Foreign and all Priority Request orders:
Call Order Entry department for price quote
at 1-916-632-4400

This chart represents the total retail price of books
only (before applicable discounts are taken).

By telephone: With Visa or MC, call 1-800-632-8676. Mon.–Fri. 8:30–4:00 PST.

By Internet e-mail: sales@primapub.com

By mail: Just fill out the information below and send with your remittance to:

PRIMA PUBLISHING

P.O. Box 1260BK

Rocklin, CA 95677-1260

www.primapublishing.com

Name_____ Daytime Telephone_____

Address _____

City _____ State _____ Zip_____

Visa /MC# _____Exp. _____

Check/Money Order enclosed for $_____ Payable to Prima Publishing

Signature_____